# I SURVIVED
## MY CHILDHOOD

YES, MIRACLES STILL HAPPEN!!

(A GUIDE FOR PARENTS OF ACCIDENT-PRONE CHILDREN)

# I SURVIVED
## MY CHILDHOOD

YES, MIRACLES STILL HAPPEN!!

(A GUIDE FOR PARENTS OF ACCIDENT-PRONE CHILDREN)

Stephen L. Franklin, Ed.D.

**ARPress**
ILLUMINATING IDEAS
EMPOWERING VOICES

**ARPress**
45 Dan Road Suite 5
Canton, MA 02021

Hotline:  1(888) 821-0229
Fax:      1(508) 545-7580

Ordering Information:
Quantity sales. Special discounts are available on quantity purchases by corporations, associations, and others. For details, contact the publisher at the address above.

Printed in the United States of America.

ISBN-13:     Softcover     979-8-89389-521-6
             eBook         979-8-89389-522-3

Library of Congress Control Number: 2024919863

TO MY PARENTS, GWENDOLYN AND JOHN FRANKLIN,

AND MY TWO SISTERS JANET AND MICHELLE,

WHO LIVED AND ENDURED WITH ME THROUGH

MY MANY ADVENTURES.

TO MY COUSIN RICHARD,

FOR BEING THE BIG BROTHER THAT I NEVER HAD.


I WOULD ALSO LIKE TO DEDICATE THIS BOOK TO ALL THE TEACHERS,

ADMINISTRATORS, NEIGHBORS, DOCTORS, NURSES, BLUE SEDANS,

TAXICABS, AND GARAGES THAT I TRAUMATIZED OVER THE YEARS.

# CONTENTS

# PROLOGUE

The inspiration behind this book arrived innocently enough, in the comforts of my bedroom. My then wife and I were just sitting around sharing some of our childhood experiences. Her stories told of life growing up in her native Colombia. Mine told of my life growing up in Washington, DC. Each time I would share one of the many stories of my childhood, her eyes would just light up with excitement and wonder. *Wonder at how I managed to survive this long!*

Claudia would often tell me how she lived her childhood through my stories, as her childhood in Colombia was so much different. She would also say that it was a miracle that I made it through my childhood. *I have to agree with her on that point!* After many such evenings and mornings of sharing our childhoods with each other, Claudia urged me to write a journal chronicling my exploits to give to the kids, I took it a step further and said maybe I should write a book. Claudia being the quiet force that she was, said, "You should. Everyone says you write well, so why not?"

Before I begin, I have to put this out as a disclaimer… I am not a professional writer. I *am* an educator. For the past twenty-six years, I have taught in the public schools of our nation; eight years in Washington, DC and eighteen years, to date, in California. I was a Social Science teacher and an English teacher before moving to the *OTHER SIDE… known as ADMINISTRATION.*

So, what would possess me to take on such a task as writing a book? *I LIKE CHALLENGES.* As Claudia frequently tells me, I am *Canson (pronounced Khan-sewn).* This is a cute way of telling me I can be a pain at times (well many times). That and the fact that several degrees later, during which countless professors, fellow students, and colleagues at work told me I wrote very well. So, I figured, what the heck.

For the record, I was not a bad kid, just mischievous. *THINGS JUST HAPPENED!*

# CHAPTER ONE

## I Was Not a Bad Kid, Just Mischievous

I was born at Washington Hospital Center in Washington, DC on January 2, 1959. This is important to note because even this simple act was eventful.

What I am about to share is the result of information being passed on to me by my parents, grandparents, and countless relatives. I say this because I do not remember being born; I had other more important things on my mind at the time... like sleep! Being born on January 2, 1959, instead of when I was *supposed* to have been born cost my parents a lot of money in terms of a tax deduction for 1958. You see, I was supposed to have been born on New Year's Eve... but  I had other plans!

My mother went into labor on New Year's Eve, *early* New Year's Eve. Everyone was assembled at our house in Washington, as they would have been for New Year's Eve, and the celebration of me being born. By everyone, I mean my parents, both sets of grandparents, a few aunts and uncles, and my sister, Janet, who was two going on three. So, everyone is at the house getting ready to party and my mother goes into labor. I can only imagine the chaos and excitement of getting me and my mother to the hospital, figuring out who was going to stay with Janet (the "baby"), etc.

My parents and I arrived at Washington Hospital Center, with grandparents in tow.

The doctor gets my mother ready and rolls her into the "Labor Room." Remember this was 1958 we are talking about, everyone is in the Labor Room, and they are checking on my mother and me, just checking away. Bright lights, tubes, monitors, things that go beep, you know, just checking. All is going well with plans being made to soon roll my mother and me into the "Delivery Room." That mysterious place that no one can go, unless you are part of the hospital staff, remember this is 1958 we are talking about. Suddenly, from what I am told, *PANIC* took over the room! The doctor got worried, which means *EVERYONE ELSE* in the room gets worried… including my mother! The doctors (there are two now), and nurses were all checking stuff (what s tuff, I don't know). All of my folks kind of got pushed to the side wondering what is going on. Have you ever noticed that when there is a *PANIC,* doctors don't answer questions? I can say this because my sister Janet (the "baby") in this part of my life, is now a doctor.

After a period of time, *PANIC* was replaced by **CALM**. The doctors, who *now* wanted to answer questions in a state of surprise, announced that I had simply decided to sleep. Yes, I, Stephen Louis Franklin (aka CANSON), in the middle of being born, decided to rethink this entire process, scared everyone in the room, and took a NAP!

I was born on January 2, 1959.

It is a good thing that I was born when I was. Growing up in the 1960s and 1970s was the perfect time for me. For a child growing up, life was easier and simpler. You had school clothes and play clothes, and you better not play in your school clothes. There were only three main TV channels; NBC, ABC, and CBS. In Washington, DC (or DC as it is often called) they were channels 4, 7, and 9. Channel 5 was a local station, now part of the Fox network, and Channel 20 required an antenna on top of the TV because it was a UHF (or was it a VHF?) station. Channel 20 is now part of the UPN network. You ate *whatever* your mother cooked; I will come back to this topic later. My mother was a very good cook; I, on the other hand, was a very picky eater.

Most importantly, the concept of child abuse was not a mainstream issue or concern. This is very important because if the awareness of child abuse had been around then as it is today… my parents would probably be under the jail. Not in the jail, they would have made a special room for them UNDER the jail. Why, you ask, because **NO ONE** would have believed it was simply ***ME doing these things to ME***!

I was an accident-prone kid. Everyone in the family kept telling my mother, "Don't worry, Gwen, he will grow out of it." It took me awhile to grow out of being accident-prone. Actually, I went through cycles in which I would suffer a series of injuries and then go for a period of time with no injuries. It was always during these periods of time in which I managed to avoid inflicting pain and suffering on myself, that the family dared to dream that I had finally outgrown being accident-prone. Those dreams proved to be false hopes. From kindergarten through the fifth grade, I had three busted heads, a fractured left wrist, got buried in a snowbank, countless bumps and bruises, and one car that *I* hit. All of this was simply me, being me! It is a miracle that I survived my childhood. I was not a bad kid, just mischievous.

My older sister, Janet, had to walk with me to school; being three years older than me, she got a reprieve when I entered the fourth grade. Until that time, I was Janet's personal albatross. I was her crazy kid brother. Again, I was not a bad kid, just mischievous. In fact, when Janet graduated from sixth grade to enter junior high school in the fall, I don't think her feet touched the ground ALL summer! She was so happy to not have to walk to school with me anymore!

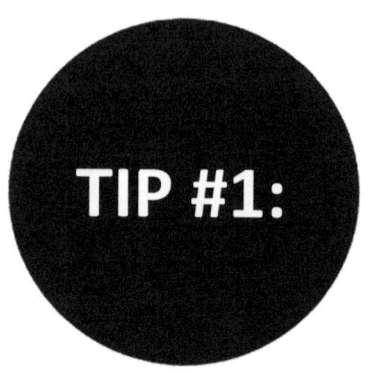

## TIP #1:

### ALL CHILDREN
### ARE A BLESSING

*All children are truly unique and special in their own right. Always expect the unexpected and accommodate your child and their unique quirks. You will be able to tell fairly early on in your child's life, if they are accident-prone. As a parent of an accident-prone child, you will have ample opportunity to embrace their unique quirks!*

# CHAPTER TWO

## 5721 Chillum Place, N.E.

5721 Chillum Place, N.E., in the upper Northeast section of Washington, DC, was not the first house we lived in when I was growing up. It was, however, the first house of my childhood where the issue was raised of whether or not I would survive my childhood.

Prior to moving to 5721 Chillum Place, N.E, we lived in a house on South Dakota Avenue, N.E. I believe the address was 2024 South Dakota Avenue; I did not bother to check the exact address with my mother or father because it was not important. Nothing happened to me there! I was a toddler and under the close watch of my parents. It wasn't until I hit kindergarten that all hell broke loose. The only real incident involving the South Dakota Avenue address was an issue surrounding a Devil's Food cake. More on that incident later.

By car, 5721 Chillum Place was only five minutes away from South Dakota Avenue, but it was an important change in school boundaries. Instead of going to Bunker Hill school where Janet started out, I began school at Keene Elementary. Keene Elementary is closed now. It is now a church or a Christian Center of some type. The District of Columbia Public Schools sold some of their excess school buildings a few years back. Being in education now, I wonder how you can have excess school buildings. Isn't the current trend to reduce class sizes? Now that I think about it, my former junior high school, Louis Charles Rabaut, was closed too. Coincidence, I think not! Perhaps if I had gone to Bunker Hill school, Keene might still be open.

The winter of 1963, Washington, DC had a rare blizzard. Growing up in Washington, DC, I can tell you that snow is a very unique phenomenon. When we would get snow, it just did not hang around for very long. The Blizzard of 1963 set its own rules. It snowed… a lot. I do not know how much snow fell, what I do recall was that you could not tell where the curb and street met. Our front lawn was like a small hill that dropped off on the way to the sidewalk. It was great for rolling down the front lawn or racing, but now it was all white. There were stairs you walked up from the sidewalk to a short landing at the top of our lawn, and then a few more steps to reach the front door stoop. But now, you couldn't see either set.

During the Blizzard of 1963, I was four years old. My father went out front to clear the steps that went from our house down to the sidewalk. All you could see was a railing sticking up through the snow where the stairs ought to be. Being four and a kid who liked to play in the snow, I wanted to help my dad shovel. After bugging my mother to let me help, she finally gave in. I had to wear a snowsuit to go outside so that I would not, "Catch my death of pneumonia."

Looking back on it now, I probably could have walked on the moon in my snowsuit. I had black rubber snow boots, the kind that had the metal latches on them that looked like mini car grills (those of you who remember, know what I am talking about). You slid the one piece through the grill, flipped it over and it was latched shut. I had on mittens, a scarf, and a knit snow hat with the flip-down ear flaps and a big pom-pom on top. The pom-pom probably saved my life.

I was now ready to go outside and help my dad shovel snow. I had on probably fifteen pounds of clothes! I could barely move, but I was ready! I grabbed my toy snow shovel, asked my mom to open the door for me, because I could not, and stepped out onto the front stoop. I called to my dad, who turned around and looked at me, at which point my mom closed the front door. I was ready to shovel snow, but my dad said to wait a minute he would come to me when he finished clearing the step he was on. I did not hear his command to wait. So, I promptly jumped down the two or three steps from the stoop to the top of the front lawn. Took two steps and WHOOSH! All I could see was WHITE! I had forgotten the front lawn sloped!

By now, my dad had finished clearing the step and turned to look for me. Of course, I was nowhere to be seen. I heard my dad call to my mom, "Gwen, did Stevie go back inside with you?" My mom said, "No, last I saw he was out there with you." At this point, the conversation shifted to where I could have gone to so fast. They called out my name. The wind was blowing, so the few footprints I had made were only faintly visible. They saw my shovel lying on top of the snow, and then they saw IT! It was the top of the white pom-pom on my snow hat.

I was not worried, I had plenty of air, I was actually quite warm, and it was cool!

I mean cool as in neat; all around me it was white and wet from my breath. I was not the least bit worried. My mom and dad on the other hand were anxious. Once they realized what had happened, it was a race to dig me out. In no time at all, the two of them using my shovel and my dad's shovel, had me out of the snowbank. They were both too frightened to fuss at me for disobeying.

After making sure I was okay, my mom took me inside, got me out of my "fifteen pounds" of clothes and fixed me some hot chocolate to warm me up. As I was drinking my hot chocolate, with the complete seriousness of a four-year-old, I asked my mom if I could go back outside and play snow cave again. I think my mom knew at that point: this boy might not survive his childhood.

The walk to Keene Elementary school from our house on Chillum Place took perhaps ten to fifteen minutes, no dawdling allowed. Dawdling was not encouraged back then. During this entire ten- to-fifteen-minute walk, I had to hold the hand of my older sister... unless of course she left me in the alley across the street from our house staring at a snarling dog that had gotten out of its yard. That's right, my older sister, my protector, I am six, and she is nine, left me in the alley crying and screaming and went on to school. When asked about it now, Janet's answer is simply, "I told you to come with me; you didn't come, so I left you." Nice!

The other side of Chillum Place had two alleys near the East and West corners. One neighbor across the street had a backyard that bordered the alley at the East end of Chillum Place. As luck would have it, this particular backyard was home to a retired police dog, who apparently was not happy about being retired. I believe the dog's name was King. King was big, black, and just flat-out mean! ALL of us kids in the neighborhood were afraid of King, and I suspect many of the adults were too. In fact, no one would cut through that part of the alley if it was known that King was out in the yard. It was worse when King actually got out of his yard, which he did from time to time. Usually, it was safe to cut through King's alley early in the morning on the way to school. You *know* the dog had to be mean to get an alley named after him.

Whose alley? King's alley!

Like I said, usually it was safe to cut through King's alley in the morning... but not this morning. You see, King had gotten out the night before, but we did not know that. King's alley was laid out like a capitol *I*. I was in kindergarten and Janet was in the third grade. We had left our house, crossed the street, and were headed to school. As luck would have it, Janet decided, being younger I had no say, to cut through King's alley.

We had walked maybe five feet into the alley, Janet was telling me to walk faster because we were running late. So naturally, I was walking slower. Suddenly, at the intersection of the "I," the biggest shadow I had ever seen (mind you I was only six) came around the corner. The shadow must have been ten feet tall! The shadow was followed by the hollow clicking of claws on concrete, and the lowest growl I had ever heard. Janet, my older sister and protector, promptly let go of my hand and began backing away. As she was backing away, she was yelling at me, *in a whisper*, to back up and come now. I heard her but I could not move! Janet kept telling me to back up as King rounded the corner of the alley. King stood there, like a gunfighter at high noon just snarling with drool dripping from his mouth.

Upon seeing this, my sister left me in the alley alone! It was just me and King. There was no one else in sight, not even a rock. Janet just left me there! She did not run back across the street to our house or to a neighbor's house.

My sister Janet Lee Franklin went on to school.

Being alone in the alley with King, I did the only thing a six-year boy could do… I wet my pants! I was also screaming and crying at the top of my lungs. I do not know why King did not put me out of my misery that morning, maybe he had already dined on some other unfortunate soul. What saved me was King's owner. He heard my screams coming from the alley and rescued me. Once he had King locked up in the house, he came back out, but I still would not move. He picked me up and carried me across the street to our house and rang the doorbell. My mother was still home, so she answered the door. King's owner pieced together the events and told my mother what had happened. My mother promptly asked where was Janet, all I could manage to say were three words, "She left me!"

I did not go to school that day.

Janet got into a whole lot of trouble, including a spanking, when she returned home from school. Janet's explanation, *"I told him to come; he didn't come, so I left him. I didn't want to get eaten too!"*

Dodge Ball was one of my favorite games when I was in kindergarten. Dodge Ball is not to be confused with Murder Ball; a hybrid version of Dodge Ball sometimes played by the upper grade kids. Upper grade in this case refers to grades 4–6. The object of Murder Ball is to take a partially deflated dodge ball, throw it as fast and as hard as possible for your age and strength, and inflict as much pain on each other as possible. In kindergarten, we played Dodge Ball.

The game of Dodge Ball for kindergarten-aged kids is totally different than it is for second- and third-grade kids. Even first graders have more arm strength and body control. For kindergartners, the object of Dodge Ball is to run around, scream a lot, and play with a ball because in kindergarten your chances of actually hitting someone with the ball are virtually ZERO.

For the teachers, the object is to allow their students to run around and burn off some of their energy.

First, there is the ball itself, a dodge ball is actually one of those huge red rubber balls that *ALL* elementary schools have, sometimes called playground balls. These balls are huge! For a child in kindergarten, it takes both hands to pick up the ball with your arms barely fitting around a fourth of the circumference. The ball is almost as big as the child holding the ball, who then attempts to raise the ball so that he or she can *try* to throw it. Anyone who has ever seen a young child try to throw one of these balls knows what I am talking about. A snail would have no problem dodging such a ball.

I say all this to simply make the point that in kindergarten, no one is at risk of *actually* being hit by the ball. I forgot this fact, and fearing for my life… I dodged the ball by running smack into the corner, the red brick corner, of Keene Elementary school. BLOOD WAS EVERYWHERE!! Children were screaming, and the teacher was probably wondering why they had to have playground duty today? Had I been looking up or in front of me, I probably would not have collided into the school building. As it was, my head was down, I was running and screaming when, BAM, the school building got in the way! I do not recall which teacher was on playground duty that day; I know that it was not my kindergarten teacher. I was taken to the school nurse, who called my mother, who in turn called my father. They came and picked me up and took me to Providence Hospital to get stitches to close the gash. This busted head, my first, occurred in March of my kindergarten year.

This visit to Providence Hospital was to be the first of many during my early childhood. I became such a "good customer," the doctors and nurses in the ER actually knew my name. Too bad hospitals do not have frequent visitor miles; I could have racked them up. My parents brought me into the Emergency Room, with me screaming and bleeding. In Emergency Rooms all across these United States, the red carpet, no pun intended, immediately gets rolled out for the suffering parents and child. Providence Hospital was no different, immediately we were taken into one of the treatment rooms. A few questions later and the doctor and nurse were ready to close the gash on my head. The nurse pulled out this HUGE curved needle, which was what they used back then, with what looked like regular sewing thread. She also pulled out an equally huge needle to inject a pain killer, so I would not feel the needle punching little holes in my scalp as they pulled the thread through.

I saw both needles and said, to myself, oh no! I jumped down off of the observation table and became a human pin ball! I had four adults in the room with me: my parents, the doctor, and a nurse, and none of them could catch me. Mind you, I am still bleeding from the gash in my scalp, but at that moment that was not a concern to me. All I saw were two huge needles, one of which was curved, and neither was going to go in me! It was all about survival! I was scooting over tables, under tables, through people's legs; faking people out left and right, head fakes, shoulder fakes. I'm telling you it was a thing of beauty; the NFL could have used my services…. Finally, they caught me. With both of my parents and the nurse holding me down, BLOOD ALL OVER THE ROOM, the doctor stitched me up. I do not know why, but the doctor and nurse suddenly were not so friendly anymore.

The rest of my kindergarten year was uneventful.

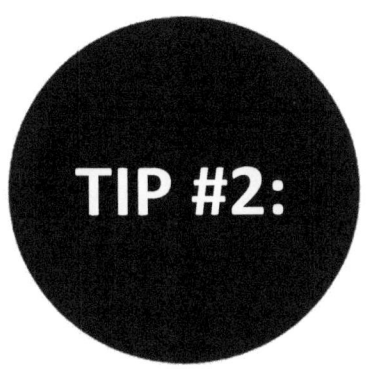

**TIP #2:**

## BRIGHTLY COLORED POM-POM

*When your child goes out to play in the snow, make sure they are wearing at least one brightly colored item. Preferably a knit snow hat with a bright pom-pom on top. My hat had a white pom-pom, so it took a moment before my parents figured out that I had sunk into the snowbank.*

*From watching years of the Science and Discovery channels, I now realize I was not in imminent danger. Snow contains a lot of air and is also quite insulating. Nonetheless, you still want to get your child out of the snowbank as soon as possible. A bright pom-pom or any bright clothing item helps!*

**TIP #3:**

## DO NOT RUN

*Hopefully, your child will never find themselves alone in an alley facing a snarling dog. However, should that happen, there are a few basic tips for survival. First, DO NOT turn and run! If you tell your child nothing else, please insist that they do not run.*

*Humans are slow, and unless there is an immediate low branch to climb, the chances of your child getting away are slim. Second, running only triggers the predatory response in an angry animal, and would likely result in increased injury.*

*So then, what should your child do? If possible, back away slowly while facing the dog. NEVER turn your back to an angry animal. If possible, climb on top of a car. Once on top of the car, call out for help. If backing away is not possible, stand as still as possible and using only their eyes, glance around at their surroundings to look for a big stick or large rock. Slowly pick up the stick or rock.*

*Tell your child to make themselves look as big as possible, wave your arms but not too aggressively as the animal may interpret that as a challenge. Finally, scream and make as much noise as possible. It will either scare the animal away, or alert others they need help.*

# CHAPTER THREE

## The Car Didn't Hit Me, I Hit It!

When I was in elementary school, they still had School Safety Patrols. I do not know when they stopped having School Safety Patrols, or why they stopped having them. It just seemed like one day they were there, and the next day they were gone, POOF! Or so it seemed.

For those of you who do not remember or who have never heard of School Safety Patrols, they were the privileged kids in elementary school. Privileged not because of money; they were privileged because they were allowed to arrive to class later than the regular kids, and leave earlier before lunch and the end of school.

Safety Patrols wore special belts that went around their waists, with a section of their belts looping over their shoulders. When fastened, their belts looked much like the shoulder and lap belts found in most cars today. When I was in kindergarten and first grade, the belts were white canvas. By the time I was in second grade, they had been upgraded to bright orange nylon/plastic type belts. Safety Patrols had badges and ranks: Patrol, Sergeant, Lieutenant, and Captain. They used to drill after school on certain days, practicing marching, military-style turns, and, most importantly, folding their belts. Safety Patrols were also the older kids, grades fourth through sixth, which meant that they were really good at bossing the younger kids around.

Safety Patrols were so special and important, the school had special days during which the Safety Patrols were allowed to wear their belts all day during class, and have special lunches. Washington, DC even had a special day called National Safety Patrol Day. Safety Patrol units would come from all over the country and take part in a big parade that marched down Constitution Avenue. Once the Safety Patrols were treated to seeing the Washington Senators baseball team, before they left to become the Texas Rangers, at DC Stadium.

I tell you all of this to point out the degree of importance given by adults to those students who were selected to be School Safety Patrols. Students who disobeyed School Safety Patrols were dealt with harshly! I was in the first grade, still living at 5721 Chillum Place, N.E. and still walking to school with my sister, Janet. I was still required to hold her hand the entire way to school, even though I am sure Janet would have preferred not acknowledging me around her friends. To get to Keene Elementary from our house, we had to cross a major street, Riggs Road twice. Riggs Road split near our house, with one section branching off down a hill to intersect with South Dakota Avenue, a huge grassy median separated the two sections. We would first cross Riggs Road at an intersection controlled by traffic lights, then turn right walking along the sidewalk that bordered the huge grassy median separating the two sections of Riggs Road. The second crossing of Riggs Road was more dangerous because there was no traffic light and cars whizzed by pretty fast as they veered off to head down to South Dakota Avenue. Due to the danger of this crossing, a Safety Patrol, sometimes two, were stationed there.

Janet and I were walking to school, I was holding her hand, and had safely navigated the first crossing of Riggs Road. I remember Janet pulling me along trying to get me to hurry up because I was walking too slowly. We then turned to walk along the sidewalk heading towards the second more dangerous crossing of Riggs Road. As we approached the corner, a Safety Patrol stepped out in front of the corner with his arms both out, which meant for us to stop until it was clear for us to cross. I KNEW what it meant when a Patrol put his or her arms out, all of us school kids knew, but I did not stop. Instead, for reasons I will never know, I pulled my hand free from Janet and ran towards Riggs Road. I got to the Safety Patrol and promptly ran under his outstretched arms... *BAM!*

I ran smack into the side door of a blue car! I cannot tell what shade of blue or what type of car it was if my life depended upon it, which miraculously it did not. I hit the car very hard, because as a kid I was pretty fast for my age. I left a nice size dent in the rear driver's door from where my hands and arms hit the car as I tried to stop myself. The driver of this car slammed on his brakes, smoking his tires, as he brought his car to a very sudden stop... which almost caused an accident. The driver of the car then hops out of his car in a panic thinking that he had hit me. He was extremely apologetic, asking if I was all right. He checked me over, offered his information to Janet and the Safety Patrol. I mean the guy was REALLY shook up!

After it was apparent that I was okay, in fact, I was in better shape than the car. I really caved in the rear door! After the driver of the car had apologized for the umpteenth time for not seeing me and hitting me, the Safety Patrol calmly said to the driver of the car, ***"No sir, you did not hit him... he hit you!"*** Janet and I were both late to school that day, as the Safety Patrol had to radio for a relief Patrol to come and then walk us to school. I was taken directly to the principal's office. Janet was given a late pass.

Going to the principal's office when I was in elementary school was the absolute LAST PLACE you wanted to be, especially for a first grader! I got lectured, fussed at, and paddled. I was given recess and lunch detention for an entire week and as if that was not enough, a note was sent home by means of Janet. I tried to forget about the amount of trouble I was going to get into when I went home that day. I spent the entire day sitting in the waiting area of the principal's office as they tried to reach my parents. Which meant by lunchtime, most of the school knew that Janet's brother was sitting in the principal's office.

I think that Janet would have preferred that she had been hit, injured, and maimed than being forced to answer countless questions about why her crazy little brother *hit* a car.

Friend: *"Janet, is it true about your brother?"*
Janet: *"Yes, it's true."*
Another Friend: *"Janet, is that your brother in the principal's office?"*
Janet: *"Yessss! Don't ask!"*
Still Another Friend: *"What did he do?"*
Janet: *"I don't want to talk about it!"* Friend: *"I feel sorry for you."*
Janet: *"Thank you."*

How did I know about the countless questions that Janet was asked? Simple! Janet made *sure* that I was aware of the amount of shame and humiliation I had heaped upon her.

I suffered my second busted head in the first grade. We used to play a game called Monkey Tag on a piece of playground equipment that we called the Monkey Bars. Many people know it as a Jungle Gym. To make sure that we are all talking or thinking about the same thing, I will clarify. The Monkey Bars looked like a three-tier wedding cake made of open steel cubes. The first tier was three levels high; the second tier was set in a little and was two levels high, with the final tier being set in still farther and was one level high.

We called them the Monkey Bars because my friends and I used to scoot over, through, and around these opens cubes very quickly, looking like little monkeys in the process. The object of Monkey Tag was to scoot over, through, and around the Monkey Bars without getting tagged, and without touching the ground. If you did, you were IT!

When I was growing up, kids were more rugged than they are now, or perhaps school officials had not thought about safety issues, as much as they do now. There were no rubber pads or mats around playground equipment as there are today. There was no rubber mat or pad around our Monkey Bars. Also, I might add, when I went to school, kids wore hard-soled shoes. You only wore tennis shoes during P.E. Hard-sole shoes also made it easier to scoot over, through, and around the Monkey Bars.

The playground equipment was set to one side of the playground with Hopscotch, Kickball, and other such games occupying the rest of the playground. There were two sets of Monkey Bars, three swing sets, a carousel, and those bars you swing from hand-to-hand on. These were all set next to a grassy slope; presumably to provide a little cushion should you fall.

One rainy day during first grade, the school's playground had been cleared for use during lunch recess—as the rain had stopped, and the sun had been out to sufficiently dry the playground. The Monkey Bars, being made of steel, took a little longer to dry and were still wet… it didn't matter to my friends and me; we wanted to play Monkey Tag. So, we did!

My friends and I were well into our game of Monkey Tag, when I became "It." As I stated earlier, hard-soled shoes made it easier to scoot over, through, and around the Monkey Bars. Wet Monkey Bars made it even easier… and slipperier. I was on the very top, outside edge of the Monkey Bars when I lost my balance. With nothing but air to grab on to, I fell backwards, spread eagled onto the grassy slope. I bounced as I busted my head. Once again BLOOD WAS EVERYWHERE!

Girls were screaming, teachers were thinking, "Why did I have to have playground duty today?" and my friends were like, "Wow, did you see him bounce!"

Once again, my parents were contacted. I think only my mother came this time. Once again, I was taken to Providence Hospital's Emergency Room. I do not think the same doctor and nurse were on duty that day. What I do recall was my mother giving me a pep talk in the car about how there was *NOT* going to be a repeat of my last visit to the Emergency Room. I think I was more afraid of my mother and what would happen if she told my father about me running around the room, than I was of those large curved needles and the sewing thread. It still took two people to hold me down, but at least I did not run around the room squirting blood everywhere… this time!

The last major injury during my first-grade year occurred at home. While going to the bathroom... I fractured my left wrist. I know it sounds crazy. How does one fracture a wrist while going to the bathroom? Trust me on this; I am a living witness that it is possible to fracture your wrist while going to the bathroom. Please allow me to explain. When I was younger, I had a fascination with monsters, as do most first graders. My fascination, though concern was a more appropriate term, with monsters was specific to the bathroom. Not anywhere else in the house; not the usual under the bed or in the closet. No, I was concerned with monsters in the bathroom. To be specific, I was concerned with monsters when you flushed the toilet. An older cousin had once told me, if you flush the toilet and it is dark, monsters will come out and get you. I can no longer remember which cousin told me this fact, but it stayed with me for a while.

We were still living at 5721 Chillum Place, N.E. when I fractured my left wrist (I emphasize my left wrist because I am left-handed, this fracture would be the first of several self-inflicted attacks on the left side of my body). My grandpop, my father's father, had come down from Pittsburgh, Pennsylvania to spend the weekend. It was Saturday morning after breakfast. Janet, my father, and Grandpop were going out somewhere, but I could not go. I was on punishment; I cannot recall what it was that I was on punishment for; all I knew was that I could not go with them.

As they were leaving, I went to my room to play with my Tonka trucks. I had quite a few Tonka trucks, some small and some quite large. Tonka had a series out at the time that was pretty huge, as toy trucks go; I think they were called the Constructors Series or something like that. They advertised them on TV with kids playing in their backyards by digging gigantic holes and hauling away tons of dirt. I had two of these large Tonka's—a dump truck and a pay loader. My room was too small for my imagination, so I moved my armada of trucks into the hallway to continue playing. Also, I might add, these Tonka trucks were made of metal.

While I was playing, my mother was busy cleaning the house, and decided it was time to wax the hallway floor. Remember, we are talking about the early '60s; people still waxed floors! To get me out of the way, my mother sent me downstairs to the basement to play. Our house on 5721 Chillum Place, N.E. was a rambler-style house, meaning that all of the living, dining, and sleeping space was on one level.

Our basement was a full basement that ran the full length of the house. Two-thirds of the basement was finished and paneled and was used for entertaining and playing. There were two doors that connected to the other third of the basement. This side of the basement was partially finished, meaning the insulation and wall board were in place, it just wasn't painted or paneled. This side of the basement had the hot water heater, the washer and dryer, my father's work room—it also had the ONLY bathroom downstairs.

While playing downstairs in the basement, I suddenly had to go! Now remember my concern about monsters and bathrooms. My mother was upstairs, and the basement door was closed, so any hope of a rescue by her was out of the question. There was a light on THAT side of the basement, the unfinished side, but to get to the door, I had to pass a dark section after I had already flushed the toilet. You can see my problem. Flushing the toilet in the dark meant the monsters were going to get me.

So, I did the only thing I could, I went upstairs to go to the bathroom, so far so good. You have to understand the floor plan of our house to understand the actions that followed. Coming up from the basement stairs, there is a short hallway that connects the kitchen and the living room depending upon which direction you turn. I could have turned left, entered the living room, made a quick right into the hallway leading to the bedrooms made another quick right and I would have been in the bathroom... safe and sound with lots of lights! Maybe ten quick steps.

I did not do that! I turned right and went into the kitchen, and because I had to go really bad, I was running! I ran through the kitchen into the dining room, turned and ran past the front door and into the living room. All the while, I was picking up speed because I had to go! I ran through the living room and was approaching the freshly waxed hallway floor. I am telling you, IT WAS **UGLY**!!! There was **NOTHING** GRACEFUL about the way I fell. I MEAN I WIPED OUT!! If you have ever watched a Road Runner cartoon, you can appreciate what I am talking about. You know when the Coyote is using his rocket powered shoes, and he falls with his arms and feet everywhere, head sticking out between his toes… just UGLY!

That was me!

I slid down the hallway, bouncing from wall to wall like a pinball. Janet's room was directly at the end of the hallway. I slammed wrist-first into the doorjamb leading to Janet's doorway. My mother, who was now in her room lying down, heard the commotion and came running out. She took one look, saw me, saw the skid mark I had left on the floor, and began fussing at me for running in the house. All the while, I was crying. I did not know that I had fractured my wrist; all I knew was that I was hurting. As I continued to cry, my mother uttered those time-honored words that parents use to quiet a crying child, *"You better stop crying before I give you something to cry about!"* I already had something to cry about, my arm was hurting. I never made it to the bathroom, the urge to go was suddenly gone… in its place was pain.

Because I did not want a spanking, I tried to stop crying, using the half-cry, half-whimper technique. My mother, who was still angry at me for messing up her floor, and who was also unaware that I had fractured my wrist, sent me to my room to wait for my father and Grandpop's return. While waiting, I continued to half cry/ half whimper at the risk of receiving a spanking. I curled up on my bed as far from my door as I could get, holding my wrist. Eventually, Janet, my father, and Grandpop returned home. My mother filled them in on my escapade, as I heard the footsteps coming down the hall; I knew I was in trouble. My father and Grandpop came in the room prepared to fuss; instead, they saw me curled up on the bed holding my wrist. My wrist by now was the size of a grapefruit. They called my mother, who came in saw my wrist and began to cry, "My baby, why didn't you tell me you had hurt yourself." *I didn't dare say what I was thinking.*

I paid yet another visit to Providence Hospital's Emergency Room, the second time that school year. The doctor, the same one from my very first visit when I ran around the room, was on duty. He remembered me!

He x-rayed my wrist to confirm the fracture and the degree of severity. He placed a cast on my arm and sent me home.

Casts in those days were not like they are today. Today casts are made from fiberglass and come in a wide range of colors. In my day, casts were made from plaster, they were sweaty, heavy, and came in one color... white, which soon turned to dirty white. I was always small for my age, and as a result, got picked on often. Here I am walking around with this club of a cast on my arm, so I decided to use it to my advantage. Suddenly I wasn't being picked on as much, at least during the eight weeks I was wearing a cast.

My teacher had to send a note home to my parents asking them to tell me to stop using my cast as a weapon.

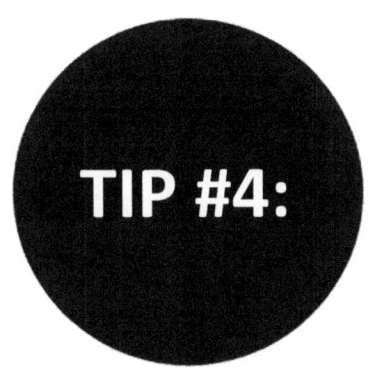

**TIP #4:**

## KEEP CALM AND CARRY ON

*Accident-prone children will have injuries, and they will do stupid things; it is simply part of their DNA. As a parent, there is precious little that you can do to prevent them from inflicting injury upon themselves. Your goal is to remain as calm as possible during these emergencies. PANIC has no place here. A parent in a state of PANIC, and an injured child are not a good combination.*

*By all means respond to the emergency call from school or your neighbor and take the call seriously. By all means be concerned for your child's well-being and safety, and get them the appropriate medical help. But PANIC? No!*

*Once you have determined that the injury is not life-threatening, take a deep breath and recognize this is just another crazy day in the life of my accident-prone child. Get to the scene as soon as you can, do not speed. Collect your child, head to the hospital, and prepare yourself for yet another long emergency room visit. Feel free to fuss as much as you need to, but panic... that's for rookies!*

# CHAPTER FOUR

## Mommy

Gwendolyn Rosetta Harewood, later Franklin, my mother, was born in Atlantic City, New Jersey. She was the sixth of seven children born to William and Edna Harewood, both immigrants from Barbados, West Indies. Being born and raised in a West Indian household, in this case a Bajan (like Cajun but with a "B," and used to refer to residents of Barbados) household was significant!

For African-Americans and many Hispanic/Latino families, there were certain rules growing up you did not dare challenge. Y'all know what I'm talking about! In a Bajan household, many of those same rules, were magnified. One could transgress if one dared, but the outcome usually was not pretty. I point this out, because my mother was a bit of a rebel growing up. Perhaps it was because my grandparents were growing tired, as she was number six of seven? Or maybe her spirit was such that it simply took much energy to constantly rein her in. Whatever the reason, my mother was able to get away with things, or say things, her siblings would not dare. I'll share some examples shortly.

This rebel spirit served my mother well, during her early school days, high school, while she attended Howard University, and later as a single parent raising three children. She was kind and supportive to many friends and family members, always willing to help or provide guidance, but she brooked little foolishness. Gwen Franklin was not to be trifled with!

Growing up, Atlantic City, was our second home as it was only a three-hour drive north from Washington, DC. Atlantic City was the family hub, this is where my maternal grandparents lived, most of my maternal aunts and uncles, and "tons" of cousins. I always had fun in "AC" as we called it, just hanging out, going up to the Boardwalk (my grandparent's house was only three to four blocks from the ocean). It was during these many trips to AC that I heard stories about Mommy as she was growing up.

Often, folks (relatives, family friends) would be sitting in the kitchen, in the living room, or on the front porch, laughing and joking, and then the stories would start! Sometimes it was an aunt or uncle, sometimes my grandparents whom we called Mom and Pop, or sometimes it was Mommy who would join in to "correct" the facts. Either way, it was a good time!

I often heard that Mommy was a bit of a tomboy, always ready to defend her brothers from any girls that gave them problems. A man should never put his hands on a woman, but back then, that rule was carved in stone!

One story that I heard repeated many times was about Mommy in high school. The story involved a girl who kept giving my Uncle Stanley a hard time. Apparently, she liked Uncle Stanley, but he didn't feel the same about her. Well, one day, she apparently had enough of her advances being turned down, and punched Uncle Stanley several times. Uncle Stanley was rightfully upset, but he did not hit her back, instead he told Mommy. A few days later, after it had rained, Mommy had Uncle Stanley point her out. Mommy jumped on that poor girl, knocked her to the ground, and then, using a stick, dug up the biggest, fattest worm she could find and would not get up off the girl until she had eaten the worm, dirt and all. After that, Uncle Stanley never had any more problems from that girl.

For that matter, girls period, were afraid to talk to Uncle Stanley because of Mommy!

Mommy grew up during the time in which school's tried to "change" students if you were not born right-handed. My mother was born left-handed. In fact, whenever my two sisters, Mommy, and I drove to AC, we represented the entire left-handed pocket of the Harewood-Greenidge family. Let me tell you the story…

The house that Mommy grew up, and still lives in to this very day, was directly across the street from New Jersey Avenue School. When my mother was growing up, the front porch was not closed in as it is now. My grandmother, Mom, would often sit on the front porch and could look into various classrooms across the street. This made it tough for getting away with things at school, but also offered an added benefit.

For weeks, Mommy's third- or fourth-grade teacher (I can't recall which) had been trying to get her to change to her right hand. Mommy refused! Mommy would say something like, *"God made me left-handed, why should I change for you?"* Bold words for the time period, we're talking the early 1940s. Apparently this one day her teacher had enough of Mommy's sass and got out her ruler. She was determined she was going to make her right-handed! Whenever she came around and saw my mother using her left hand, she would whack her across the hand with her ruler. This went on for a while, until Mommy, out of reflex grabbed the ruler. Big mistake!!

The teacher then grabbed Mommy out of the seat and started to hit her with the ruler. As luck would have it, Mom, had just sat down on the front porch, could see into Mommy's classroom and saw the teacher hitting her. Mom got up, crossed the street, entered the school, and marched right into the classroom. Mom in her thick Bajan accent bellowed,

*"Don't ye lay anuddah hand on dat chil'. You ain't she muddah, what that chil' do that cause ye to strike she so?" (In the West Indian English dialect, the "th" sound doesn't exist, so another becomes anuddah, mother becomes muddah).*

Needless to say, the teacher and class were shocked! The teacher explained that Mommy was being sassy, explained the situation and that Mommy had not followed her instructions to switch hands. Mom had heard enough,

*"Don't make me vex, ye sayin' they're sometin' wrong wit she cause she off hand? I the muddah, if I okay, wit she off hand, then you best be okay wit she off hand. Don't ye strike she no more over foolishness!"*

Mommy remained left-handed and passed on that trait to my two sisters and myself.

Mommy was the first in her family to attend college, she was accepted into Howard University in Washington, DC. Washington, DC in the early 1950s like many areas in the south was struggling with racial issues. Washington, DC or "Chocolate City" as it would come to be called, did not emerge from its racial issues for another ten years or so. Having grown up in very tight-knit West-Indian-influenced community in small-town Atlantic City, Mommy was in for some eye-opening experiences.

Mommy often tells of her first true experience with blatant racism while attending Howard University. Mom had sent Mommy some money for her birthday and told her to go and buy herself something nice. Mommy went downtown with one of her friends from Howard to one of the big department stores; I cannot recall if it was Woodward and Lothrop (Woodies as it was often called) or Garfinkel's. After looking around, Mommy found several dresses and asked to try them on. The clerk informed Mommy, very coldly, *"We don't let niggers try on clothes here."* Mommy, angry, insisted that she does not buy clothes that she cannot try on. The clerk repeated her comment and refused to let Mommy try on the dresses. The friend who was with Mommy said, *"Let's go, Gwen, I'll explain later."*

Mommy and her friend left without further incident. Once outside, Mommy's friend explained that is just how it is here at certain stores. You have to get used to it. Mommy said, "I don't want to get used to it. How can I buy clothes if I can't try them on to see how they look and fit?" Mommy and her friend went to another store, and had a similar incident. Disheartened, they returned to Howard's campus. Later that day, Mommy called Mom in AC, crying, and explained that she was going to send the money back because she can't buy anything here.

Barbados was a British colony up until its independence in 1966. This incident occurred in the early 1950s. Unbeknownst to Mommy,

Mom had called the British embassy in Washington, DC to complain about the incident and how her daughter was being treated…

As I write this, now I see where Mommy got her rebellious streak from…

A few days later, a big black limousine pulls up to her dorm on the Howard campus. It was common for the big-name Black entertainers of the day to perform at the Howard theater or come onto campus when they were in town. So here is this big limousine, and everyone is trying to guess who is in the car. Suddenly, Mommy hears her name being called over the intercom to come down to the dorm's lobby. Mommy and several of her friends come down, curious, giggly, wondering who was in the car and why do they want Gwen Franklin?

Mommy is greeted by a British gentleman who asks if she is Gwendolyn Harewood? Mommy says yes, to which the gentlemen explained that your mother called the British embassy about an incident that occurred a few days ago. He went onto explain that the "car" out front was for her, and if she is willing, they could go and resolve the matter.

Mommy and the friend who was with her got into the back seat of the limousine, giggling as they drove off towards downtown. The limousine parked out in front of the store, the gentleman opened the door, and Mommy and her friend got out. The gentleman explained that Mommy was to go back to the same department, pick out whatever she liked and insist upon trying on the clothes. He explained that he would be present, but wait in the background until he needed to step forward.

Mommy and her friend, nervous but emboldened, went inside and encountered the same woman from a few days ago. The clerk, indignant that Mommy had returned, said, "I told you before, we don't let niggers try on clothes here." The British gentleman then stepped forward, identified himself and said, *"These two young ladies are British subjects, unless you want an international incident, I suggest you allow them to try on whatever they desire."* The clerk turned and looked at her manager, who nodded, and allowed both Mommy and her friend to try on whatever they chose. After trying on a few items, Mommy walked to the counter with several items, laid them down, and said, *"I don't think I like anything here after all."* The clerk was noticeably upset, but could do or say nothing. The British gentleman thanked the clerk for her time, and they all left. Gwen Franklin was not to be trifled with!

Mommy met my father during her time at Howard University. My father was in the Army and was stationed at Fort Myer in Washington, DC. They married, and first had Janet and then yours truly. By the time I was in the third grade, my parents had divorced. Life changed drastically for all of us after the divorce, something that will be explained in further detail in the following chapters.

As a single mother with two children, and a third soon to arrive, Mommy had some very clear rules and expectations. Being late to school, even if we lived all the way across town, was not an option. Janet and I, from junior high on had the task of starting dinner, based upon who got home from school first. Our task was to get dinner started, change out of our school clothes and get started on our homework. Dinner did not have to be finished by the time Mommy got home, but it better be started!

At the time, it was a lot of pressure depending upon who person number two was through the door. If person number two was Janet or vice versa, you could say come on, I forgot. If Mommy was person number two, and sometimes she was, there was nothing to talk about… you were in trouble! Looking back now, I am happy for that experience, as I am now a very good cook.

Mommy has always been involved in education administration for as long as I can remember. First as Regional Director for the Washington area, Boys and Girls Club, and later as an administrator at Delaware State College (now University). She served on an education council under President Jimmy Carter; to this day she still has a picture of her and President Carter. I will never forget one evening the phone rang while we were living at 712 Alabama Ave. S.E., it was the White House Operator. Thinking it was one of my friends playing a joke, I said, "Yeah sure," and hung up. A few moments later, the phone rang again, it was the White House Operator calling for Mrs. Gwen Franklin, and again I said, "Stop playing" and hung up.

The phone rang again, this time the operator said, this really is the White House do not hang up. Like any level-headed teenager, I froze, put the phone on the counter and ran to the stairs and yelled *"Ma! It's the White House, why is the White House calling here?"* Mommy said, *"Boy, stop yelling"* and told me to hang up after she picked up the phone. So of course, I listened for a few moments before hanging up... it was President Carter my mother was speaking to!

From an early age, I knew that attending college was an expectation, not an option.

It was not a matter of *if* I was going to college, but rather *where* I was going to college. My mother attended Howard, so I could have gotten in fairly easily. My father worked at George Washington University, so I could have attended for next to nothing. I had other ideas, I simply wanted to get out of DC! Ball State University in Muncie, Indiana was about as diametrically opposed to Washington, DC as one could get. I went from the metropolis alternately known as "Chocolate City or CC" to rural Muncie, Indiana. Instead of being among the many, I was among the few; 900 minority students on a campus of 18,000.

My first incident of blatant racism occurred while at Ball State. That is not to say that all of my experiences at Ball State were negative, most were not. This one incident, however, left a "mark" on me. I was a freshman in September 1977. The TV show *Roots* had just premiered, and overnight I went from Stephen to being called "Toby."

One Friday evening, a few days after the premiere of *Roots*, I was in my dorm lobby shooting pool with my roommate and two friends from the room next to ours. All three: Gary, Lowell, and Jeff were white, with two being from southern Indiana near the Kentucky border. We were enjoying ourselves, having some fun. A bunch of guys from the third floor came down insisting that they wanted to use the pool table. The student desk clerk explained the table was in use, and that they would have to wait for us to finish. Apparently waiting, plus the fact that they had been drinking, was not an option. There were several guys, but the one who stood out was a guy named Dave Wozny (I probably have misspelled his last name), began yelling at us to get off the table.

We ignored them and kept on playing. Dave aimed his taunts at me yelling; "Hey, Toby, get off the table we want to play." This went on for a few moments, with all of us wondering who are they talking to, there is no one named Toby over here. After a few more taunts, with a few "N" words thrown in, it became clear they were talking specifically to me. A few of Dave's friends joined in calling me types of "N" I had never heard before. While all of this is happening, I'm looking at my roommate and friends, noticing I am the only Black person down here, and these three guys aren't saying anything in my defense. I'm looking at three white guys here, and about four to five over there; this is not good!

I took my pool cue, flipped it around so that I am holding the pool cue like a baseball bat. I backed into a corner and was prepared to start swinging if necessary. Apparently, my backing into a corner snapped my roommate and friends, **and** the desk clerk out of their "fog." My roommate said leave me alone, he isn't bothering anyone, and the desk clerk called the dorm director. The situation was defused and I ran to my dorm room and locked the door. I remember calling Mommy, crying serious tears, and insisting that I wanted to come home, **NOW!** Mommy got me to calm down and tell her what happened. I kept saying but these guys were my friends, just the other day I played ball with them. Mommy, in all of her wisdom, said, *"Those guys were never your friends, it took a TV show and some beer and alcohol, but now you know where they're coming from and what they really think."*

I kept saying Mommy, *"I want to come home. I don't want to stay here anymore."* To snap me out of it, my mother yelled at me! "Stephen," she said, "you listen to me. *If you start running now, you will be running for the rest of your life. I will not have my son running from no one! You wanted to go to that school; now you are going to stay at that school, at least for this year. After that we can talk about transferring."*

I graduated from Ball State in 1981.

While hard to hear at the time, Mommy was right. I have since repeated a version of her declaration to my own son.

To put it simply, my mother is truly a remarkable woman.

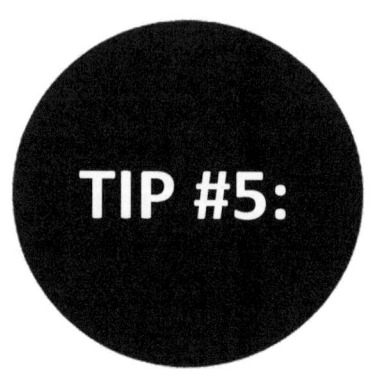

## TIP #5:

## PARENT FIRST, FRIEND SECOND

*As a parent, you will often have to take a stand on difficult topics, which your child will not agree with. That is okay, your job is to first be the parent... not the friend. (There will be plenty of opportunities for you to be friends with your child.) Your child will be angry and upset with you, they may even say "I hate you," that is okay. As parents, we often have to take the hard stand on difficult topics.*

*The incident I recounted at Ball State, I was so angry with my mother when I hung up. I was furious! I thought she did not understand the gravity of the situation; I thought she did not hear me. She heard me all right. My mother, however, knew something that I did not. Running from difficult situations doesn't make the problem go away. She knew I had to learn how to face and deal with racism and similar difficult situations, particularly as a young Black male.*

*Regardless of race or gender, learning how to deal with difficult situations is a vital life lesson. This is a lesson all children and young adults must learn. As a retired high school principal, I have seen firsthand the results of parents who try to be the friend first, instead of the parent.*

*Whenever I conducted a parent-teacher conference, I could quickly determine who was in charge in that particular household.*

*When you choose to emphasize friendship first, instead of having a child, who respects and listens to you. The result is a child who openly disrespects you and disregards you.*

# CHAPTER FIVE

## "Keep Him Quiet; We'll be There When We Finish Eating"

I did not inflict any pain or suffering on my body in the second grade. Family members, most importantly my parents were beginning to think, believe, hope, and pray that I had finally outgrown being accident-prone. They were wrong! I was just taking a break... no pun intended.

Whenever I injured myself, I had a knack for interrupting quiet time or meals. By the time I entered the third grade, my parents were seasoned veterans at dealing with Stephen-related emergencies. Seasoned veterans, almost professionals at dealing with me and my various emergencies, like fire fighters responding to a call. Panic had been replaced by purposefulness. My father yelling out orders like a fire captain.

*"Gwen, you grab the hose, I'll get the axe and check the upper floors."*

*"Janet, you monitor the flow gauges, make sure we are getting good pressure on the hoses."*

Not that my parents and Janet didn't care; it had simply become routine. Getting a call from the school or neighbor about me injuring myself was *not* a big deal anymore. Instead of chaos and panic, the goal now was to keep me quiet until they got there!

During the third grade, four major things happened to me. Three of which I will talk about in this chapter. When I was a child, I used to like to see things burn. Ants under a magnifying glass, cigarette butts in an ashtray, paper in an ashtray, etc. You get the point. I guess it was because my parents made sure that Janet and I were aware of the dangers of fire. Even the schools and television joined in through use of Smokey the Bear and his pal Woodsy Owl. I was not a danger to myself or anyone for that matter, I was just curious.

We were still living at 5721 Chillum Place, N.E. when I accidentally tried, to set the bathroom on fire. This is the same bathroom, that I never made it to when I fractured my left wrist. I say accidentally because I really did not mean for the fire to burn so quickly; I was just curious as to what would happen. There was a blackout in our neighborhood. I cannot recall the reason for the blackout, just the fact that when I opened the kitchen door and looked out all you saw was darkness! No streetlights, nothing! My parents were ready and prepared for just such an emergency, out came the flashlights and candles. At first it was kind of cool, it was like camping out at home. Janet and I got our blankets and came into the living room. My mother made hot chocolate with marshmallows for Janet and I; she made coffee for her and my father.

She made a plate of sandwiches, making sure to keep the cold air in the refrigerator… you know what I am talking about. Now that we had food and something to drink, my parents began to tell Janet and I, stories about growing up in the Depression era, my father fighting in the Korean War, etc. Basically, anything to keep our minds off of the fact the lights were out and that there was no television. Actually, it was not too bad sitting in the dark, my mother had two boxes of emergency candles and one flashlight. Sitting in the living room with candles flickering was actually soothing.

The lights tried to flicker back on after a while, so my father took the one flashlight and went downstairs to the basement to check the fuse panel. As luck would have it, I suddenly had to go to the bathroom while my father was downstairs. There was **NO WAY** I was going to go down the hallway or go to the bathroom in the dark. Remember, I had "a thing" about bathrooms and the dark, which was how I fractured my wrist in the first place.

My mother tried to get me to wait until my father came upstairs from the basement with the flashlight. I could not wait. When an eight-year-old tells you he has to go… he has to *GO!* My mother offered to walk me to the bathroom, but I declined her offer trying to be a big boy. My mother walked me to the beginning of the hallway and cautiously handed me a candle holder telling me to be very careful as I walked with the lit candle, and to leave the bathroom door open. For some reason, my mother emphasized my **WALKING** with the lit candle. I went into the bathroom and placed the candleholder with the lit candle on top of the toilet (the tank part that holds the water). For a moment, I forgot I had to go to the bathroom; I was so amazed at the shadows the flickering flame made on the walls. My mother calling to me, asking if everything was okay broke me out of the trance, so I sat down and did my thing.

We had a metal trashcan next to the toilet that happened to have pieces of tissue and other paper in it. I took a few pieces (this was before I flushed the toilet) lit them and then quickly dropped them into the toilet. I got a little bolder, and took a fresh piece of paper, twisted it, lit it, held it for a moment and then dropped it into the toilet. My mother, who was still at the beginning of the hallway (remember I had not flushed the toilet yet), called to me saying; "What is that smell, is something burning?" Of course, I said, "Oh it's nothing" and then flushed the toilet. I think my mother relaxed when she heard me flush the toilet, because I heard her go sit down on the couch in the living room. I washed my hands and was about to leave the bathroom when an idea popped into my head. *What would happen if I lit a piece of toilet paper and put it in the trashcan?* So, I did, and left the bathroom with my candleholder and candle.

My father came upstairs from the basement a little while later. As he was passing the hallway coming into the living room, he noticed a light coming from the bathroom. My father said, "Gwen, what is that light coming from the hall bathroom? Is something burning?" Both of my parents ran down the hall to the bathroom, the metal trashcan was a huge fireball! The wall next to the trashcan was blackened with the wallpaper just starting to catch fire. My father, somehow, grabbed the trashcan and threw it into the tub and turned on the faucet, my mother meanwhile splashed water from the toilet onto the wall. Once the fire was out, my parents turned and looked at me, before they could even ask what happened, I cracked! Tears were just streaming down my face!

*"I didn't mean to light the toilet paper on fire and throw it into the trashcan… it was an accident!"*

I got the second worst spanking of my life (the worst would come years later in Chapter Seven), for almost setting the house on fire, and for causing my father to burn his hand. I was "on punishment" for two weeks, which meant school and home, no playing outside, no television, no friends coming over, just school and home.

Janet, who was standing in the hallway when I confessed my crime, just shook her head with a look on her face somewhere between disgust and I cannot believe what this boy just did. Janet also made sure to "rub it in" each day for the two weeks that I was "on punishment."

I never burned anything after that incident.

My third busted headed occurred when I was attending a birthday party for my buddy Paul. Paul lived across the street from 5721 Chillum Place, N.E. at the other end of the "I" of "King's Alley." Paul and I were in the third grade together; he had just turned eight, and it was going to be a big party. All of his friends from school were invited, and since I was his best friend, I was invited first. If I remember correctly, the party was in early October. I say October because we were going through "Indian Summer" at the time. For those who do not know what "Indian Summer" is, it is a brief period lasting two to three weeks during autumn when the weather and temperatures get very warm as if it's summer.

Back in those days, getting invited to a birthday party was a BIG event. You didn't dress up in sneakers and jeans, oh no! You got dressed up; I mean you showed up *CLEAN!!* Remember this was a time period, the early sixties, in which you had school clothes and play clothes, nowadays school clothes *ARE* play clothes. I wore a short suit to Paul's party, not a short set, but a short suit. A short suit was a regular suit, but instead of having the regular long pants, it came with short pants. I wore a white dress shirt and a clip-on bow tie with dress shoes, I was *CLEAN!!* Janet who was three years older had been asked by Paul's mother if she could help with serving the younger children. Janet and I walked across the street, with me holding her hand, and arrived at Paul's house.

You have never seen so many perfectly dressed eight- and nine-year-old boys and girls in one place as there were at Paul's party. Of course, two hours later, it was a totally different story! After about one hour, we had gone outside to play some game in Paul's backyard involving a playground type ball (you know, the big red kind that are very soft, and have the little raised ridges for grip). By this time, my jacket had come off and was inside Paul's house, and my shirt tail was hanging out, I didn't know where my bowtie was, though I think I gave it to Janet, but no matter what, I was having fun! We were playing with the ball when it sailed over the fence into Paul's neighbor's backyard. I quickly volunteered to climb over the fence and get the ball. If Janet had seen me, I would have gotten in trouble for climbing in my good clothes. But she was not in the backyard at the time, so I climbed over.

I had retrieved the ball and had thrown it back into Paul's yard. I was beginning to climb back over the fence, *without being detected*, when Janet came out. I was BUSTED!! Janet had a tray of plastic cups filled with fruit punch she was going to pass out. Instead of hurrying across the fence and trying to "play it off," I froze, trying to hide on the neighbor's side of the fence, hoping she would not see me. She did, and immediately came over to the fence and started fussing at me, telling me she was telling Mommy about me climbing in my good clothes.

I started crying, saying I was sorry and asking her not to tell. At this point, I continued to climb over the fence, and I was balanced on the very top bar of the fence, crouched so I could jump down into Paul's yard. I was holding the top bar with my hands on either side of me. As Janet was fussing at me, she made a gesture that I took as her reaching out for me, so I let go of my hold on the top bar. Janet did not have me in her grasp; I lost my balance and immediately fell backwards into the neighbor's yard. *BAM!* I hit my head on one of those huge stones used for creating decorative borders along fences. Blood was everywhere!! Janet was calling for Paul's mother, another parent who was there came running over, and several of the girls were screaming! Basically, it was pandemonium. My white shirt was now hopelessly covered with blood, Janet was mad at me, and Paul's mother was frantic.

They, I cannot tell you who they were, took me upstairs to one of the bedrooms and gave me a bunch of towels to hold to my busted head. They took off my blood-soaked white shirt and gave me one of Paul's old T-shirts to wear. They also wiped my face and neck with a clean wet cloth. Paul's mother had Janet call over to our house, my mother answered, Janet very smugly told her the news about me busting my head again, and then promptly passed the phone to Paul's mother.

Paul's mother, who was a rookie at these kinds of things, was very upset and panicky. I remember that she kept apologizing for what had happened and told my mother she needed to hurry. My mother asked her how I was doing; Paul's mother said that I was sitting up quietly on the bed. She said that she'd given me one of Paul's shirts to wear and offered to replace the blood-stained shirt. My mother apparently said thank you, but don't worry about it, that it was not her fault. I say apparently, because I saw Paul's mother visibly relax. My mother again asked how I was doing, Paul's mother said he is doing fine, but you need to hurry.

To this last statement, my mother, the savvy veteran of Stephen emergencies, uttered those now famous words…

*"Keep him quiet; we'll be there when we finish eating."*

I know this because Paul's mother had a very perplexed look on her face as she turned to face myself and others in the room. One of the other mothers asked, and Paul's mother repeated my mother's statement, adding that my mother and father had just sat down to eat and that they would be over in about twenty minutes!

My mother and father finally *walked* across the street, and I was off to pay yet another visit to Providence Hospital's emergency room. By now, I was used to the process of stitching busted heads, so I did not run around the room or create a fuss. Or maybe, I had just lost too much blood? The one thing that sticks out in my mind about this entire incident, I did not get any cake or a goody bag.

The third major event that occurred in third grade was my parents getting divorced. My mother, Janet, and I moved across town to the lower Northeast section of Washington, DC. to 42nd Street and Benning Road, N.E. We lived in that apartment until I finished elementary school. By the time I was entering junior high school, we had moved back into a house. My father was still in the picture pretty much until I began junior high school, then he just POOFED!! Both of my parents have varying explanations, all I truly know is that my father did not come back into my life until I was thirty-two years old. Things are fine now between him, Janet, and me. He is definitely a part of our lives, and my family's life now

## TIP #6:

## TAKE SEVERAL DEEP BREATHS

*There will be countless times when your accident-prone child will do something that makes you want to kill him or her. No matter how angry you are, no matter how crazy or dangerous the stunt that your child pulled... do NOT kill them!*

*First, it is illegal and second, it is illegal.*

*In these moments, take a deep breath, or several deep breaths, count to ten... or maybe one hundred if you need to. After your blood pressure has come down, and the vein on your forehead has receded, then deal with the issue.*

*Patience! Patience is the point I am highlighting here. Feel free to: punish, fuss, scold, ground them for life, maybe a spanking if you deem it appropriate... just take a deep breath first.*

**TIP #7:**

FOR FREQUENT AND RECURRING
SELF-INFLICTED INJURIES,
PLEASE REFER TO TIP #4.

# CHAPTER SIX

## "They Lied"

Moving across town to the lower Northeast section of Washington, DC, was the beginning of many changes in my life.

The first was school itself. My mother wanted Janet and me to continue attending Keene Elementary in our old neighborhood. To achieve this feat, Janet and I had to catch the city bus, actually two city buses to get to school. This twice daily cross-city trek did not end with elementary school; it continued until Janet and I graduated from high school. By high school, the daily commute to school now involved three buses. When I caught the city bus in the third grade, it was known as D.C. Transit. By the time I graduated from high school the city bus had changed its name to Metrobus.

With all of this cross-city commuting Janet and I went through daily, being late to school was *NOT* an option. Suddenly, Janet and I had very tight schedules in the mornings and afternoons. We had to be out the door by a certain time or we *would* be late to school. We also had to be home by a certain time after school ended. At first, adjusting to our new schedules was difficult, and often made us weary, due to the extra 1½–2 hours added to our day on each end. But a miraculous thing happened as a result of our daily cross-town travels—Janet and I became closer. Instead of Janet being the bossy older sister and me being the annoying younger brother, Janet and I became simply brother and sister. Janet and I rode the bus together until she began high school and I began junior high school.

The second major change involved making new friends. Janet and I still had our old friends and would sometimes spend the weekends at their houses, but with us living across town, we could not do that very often. So, making friends was a new challenge. Perhaps it was because I could only spend time with my old friends at school that I became extremely talkative during class time; needless to say, this created a problem. I had several notes sent home from my teacher during the last semester of third grade. Until one day, talking began to become painful.

My throat started off becoming a little raspy, similar to most ordinary sore throats. So, my mother, thinking it was just a regular cold used the tried-and-true home remedy of gargling with salt water and rubbing Vick's Vapor Rub on my throat and chest. That seemed to work at first, but then my throat began to get progressively sorer and I began to run a slight temperature. My mother took me to an Ear, Nose, and Throat Specialist who diagnosed me with tonsillitis.

Now I heard about tonsillitis from some of my classmates and I knew it meant I had to go to the hospital and have some type of surgery. Going to the hospital did not initially frighten me, I mean I was already a veteran of several hospital visits, so what was one more? Now the surgery thing, that was NEW!

The doctor, sensing my concern, explained the procedure to my mother and me. Then the doctor told ***the biggest lie known to mankind***, he told me after the surgery my throat would be just a ***little*** sore!

He then told me how part of the after-surgery care meant that I would be allowed to eat as much ice cream, Jell-O, apple sauce, and ginger ale as I wanted to in order to soothe my throat. When he told me that, I was ready to have the surgery that SAME day! To tell me, a nine-year-old that I could eat *ALL* the ice cream, Jell-O, apple sauce, and ginger ale I wanted and my mother couldn't say anything…? Those were the magic words. I was actually looking forward to the surgery, just so I could hurry up and get to the post-op foods.

46

The day of the surgery came. I checked into Children's Hospital with my mother. The nurses even commented on the fact that I was in such good spirits. All I was thinking about was ice cream, Jell-O, apple sauce, and ginger ale. I was like Dorothy from the *Wizard of Oz* instead of "Lions, Tigers and Bears, oh my!" I was thinking, "Ice cream, Jell-O, and apple sauce, oh yeah!" When it was time for my surgery, the doctor and the nurse came to my room, spoke with my mother and me, and they wheeled me down the hall. My mother could accompany me to the pre-op room, where she held my hand as the nurse placed what looked like a balloon to my mouth and told me to first breath in, and then try to blow up the "balloon." I did this two or three times… I don't remember falling asleep.

I woke up in my hospital room with my throat on **FIRE!!** My throat hurt so much I didn't want to swallow my *saliva*… much less ice cream, Jell-O, apple sauce, or ginger ale. For one full week, it felt like someone had lit and blown up an entire pack of firecrackers in my throat. My mother had to fight with me to get me to swallow just about anything. By the second week, my throat was still sore and it still hurt to swallow, but at least now I could finally get my reward. For the next two weeks that I was home from school, I was one happy nine-year-old. Ice cream, Jell-O, apple sauce, ginger ale, warm soup, apple juice, I was in "hog heaven."

I finally returned to school three weeks after my surgery. On my very first day back to school after my surgery, my teacher sent a note home, "I realize that Stephen has just had his tonsils taken out and probably could not talk very much after the surgery. But could you please ask him to not "make up for lost time" during class?"

**TIP #8:**

## DON'T LIE

*If your child is scheduled to have any type or surgery, without scaring him or her, level with them about the procedure. Let them know what to expect after the surgery, how long they might be in pain, etc. Children are a lot stronger emotionally than we adults like to admit.*

*For example, tonsillitis is a fairly common childhood illness. For the doctor to say that my throat would be "just a little sore afterwards," and for my mother to go along with it. That was the biggest lie known to mankind! I was excited, that is true, about the prospect of eating apple sauce, Jell-O, and drinking ginger ale. I would have also appreciated knowing that for the first week my throat would be extremely sore. If I had known the details ahead of time, I could have mentally prepared myself.*

# CHAPTER SEVEN

## Daddy

My father was born John Louis Franklin, III in Pittsburgh, Pennsylvania. He was the second of three children born to John Louis Franklin, Jr. and Helen Talbot Franklin.

I emphasize the genealogical order of my father and grandfather, because I almost became John Louis Franklin, IV. Had it not been for my mother forbidding it, I would have. Her reasoning, we have enough John Franklin's for one family, "Let the boy have his own name." Instead, I became Stephen Louis Franklin, I (just kidding), simply Stephen Louis Franklin!

I have always disliked the notion of Jr., IIIs, and such. Life is challenging enough, why start off life carrying someone else's name and their accompanying triumphs and failures. I think everyone should be able to blaze their own path anew. Maybe I inherited that belief from Mommy while waiting to be named? Okay, enough proselytizing.

Daddy had two siblings, Aunt Marjorie and Uncle Walter, with Uncle Walter being the youngest. Prior to my parents divorcing, Janet and I would split time during the summer between Pittsburgh and Atlantic City. To avoid confusion, we called our maternal grandparents, Mom and Pop, and our paternal grandparent, Grandmom and Grandpop. A note about Grandmom, Daddy's biological mother died when Janet was very young, and before I was born. The woman I knew as Grandmom, Mabel Franklin, was Grandpop's second wife.

That said, Janet and I grew up in a warm loving family, with love and attention from both sides of the family. On the Harewood-Greenidge side of the family, Janet and I (and later Michelle), were among the many grandchildren. On the Franklin side of the family, Janet and I were two of four grandchildren. Uncle Walter had two girls, Lynne and Paula. Aunt Marjorie chose to become a "career woman," as a city librarian and never married or had children. Whenever we went to Pittsburgh, we usually stayed at Aunt Marjorie's house, along with her cousin Uncle Reggie (Talbot). Aunt Marjorie was not a great cook, so often we would eat out… which was fine with us! Howard Johnson's cafeteria was one our favorite places to go eat. Often, we would go over to Uncle Walter's, where Aunt Lois would fix dinner. Either way it was a fun time!

Two things I liked about visiting Pittsburgh was McEntyre's Bakery, and Kennywood Park! I am not sure if McEntyre's is still around or not, but they made the best, soft, fruit-filled cookies ever! The cookies were soft, light to medium brown, and with either cherry, apricot, raisin, or one other filling. Man! They also made these pinwheel cookies, but the fruit-filled cookies were some kind of good!! Whenever we would visit Pittsburgh, two trips to McEntyre's were made, one shortly after we arrived and another to bring two dozen assorted fruit-filled cookies with us back to D.C.. My favorites were the cherry and apricot. Daddy and Uncle Reggie loved the raisin filled.

Kennywood Park was the first amusement park I ever visited. There was a children's section with less scary rides, and the main park with the bigger rides. I was surprised when I found out recently that Kennywood is still alive and well.

Uncle Reggie was a cool uncle; he smoked Dutch Masters cigars, and always had wonderful stories to tell. Janet and I knew him as a house painter/carpenter. It wasn't until many, many, years later that we found out Uncle Reggie was a retired mathematics professor from Lincoln University in Jefferson City, Missouri. Apparently, mathematics and science ran in the Franklin-Talbot family… that gene obviously skipped me (but I digress)! Our Uncle Walter Talbot lived in Baltimore, Maryland and was the mathematics department chair at Morgan State University. The mathematics building is now named in his honor.

Perhaps because of Uncle Reggie, or perhaps because Lincoln University was one of the closest Historically Black Colleges and Universities (HBCUs) to Pittsburgh, Daddy and his two siblings all attended Lincoln University. Daddy majored in Chemistry; there it is, that math and science thing again!

Shortly after leaving Lincoln University in 1952, Daddy enlisted in the US Army and served during the Korean War. He obtained the rank Specialist Second Class before enrolling in Officer Candidate School. He was honorably discharged in 1958, as a Second Lieutenant. It was while stationed at Fort Myer in Washington, DC that he met Mommy, and the rest, as they say, is history.

Unlike Mommy's side of the family, I know little about Daddy growing up. I've heard a few college stories, but not too much else. Growing up, for as long as I can remember, Daddy always had two jobs. His main job was working at George Washington University, where he taught and ran the biochemistry lab for medical students. I remember one of the part-time jobs he had when we lived on 5721 Chillum Rd. It was a weekend job at a research lab, and he referred to it as "The Mouse House." I do not recall his exact duties, but I think it had to do with monitoring the lab mice, make sure they were fed, and still alive. On several occasions he would take me with him. It was kind of cool and gross, all at the same time. I do not recall specifically what they were testing, but I think it had to do with cancer research?

Daddy always had a booming voice, no need for a microphone… ever! Whenever I was outside playing, and he would call for me, it felt like the ground was shaking! I could always tell how much trouble I was in by how many names were used to call me. *"Stephen"* was just normal— time to eat, time to go, time to come in, etc. *"Stephen Franklin,"* was a bit more serious, *"Stephen Louis Franklin,"* meant just dig the hole now, because I'm dead! Later on, Mommy adopted a similar method.

Daddy was very "black and white" about things, maybe it was his military background, or his chemistry mind. Whatever the reason, Daddy would allow you to explain, but the majority of the time it did not change the outcome. *"Did you or did not you not, run down the hall, after your mother told you no running in the house? Did you or did you not, accidentally, on purpose, light paper in the bathroom and almost burn down the house?"* Okay… I deserved to get in trouble for these incidents, but there were countless others, less severe but with the same inquisition. That said, there were plenty of times of Daddy was pretty cool.

Often, he and his buddies would come over and watch football. Daddy would pretend to not see me sneak a sip, or two of his beer. Ironically, beer back then tasted good, but as an adult I have never acquired a taste for the beverage. The first baseball game I attended was in Pittsburgh at Three Rivers Stadium with Daddy and Uncle Walter (Franklin). The Pirates were playing someone, I cannot even recall if they won or not. All I knew was the hot dogs, soda, and peanuts tasted exceptionally good that day!

After my parents divorced, Daddy was still around, just not as much in the picture. At least two weekends each month, I would go hang out with Daddy at his apartment, and do guy stuff. Nothing extraordinary, just hanging out. Gradually the twice per month became once per month, and then finally after we moved to 712 Alabama Ave., S.E., they stopped all together. Daddy just POOFED! We knew where he lived, and he knew where we lived, he just wasn't around.

Daddy reentered my life when I turned 32. Apparently, Daddy had remarried and his second wife forbade him to see us, for fear he might get back together with our mother. As I stated in chapter five, both Mommy and Daddy had varying versions about what happened. This was Daddy's version. As there was no way to verify the events, or change them, I accepted his explanation (as did Janet), and we attempted to move forward.

Filling a twenty- to twenty-one-year gap was difficult, but we moved forward as best we could. There was no point in dwelling on what could not be undone. Though unspoken, I think Daddy felt guilty about the missed years, you could tell when he recalled stories of us growing up. Often his stories about us were trapped in the time period on 5721 Chillum Place.

It made it difficult buying birthday and Father's Day cards, as the sentiments expressed did not match my experience. Perhaps it was because of the gap, that I had a strong desire to understand Daddy; what made him tick, how he thought, what his hobbies were. To my knowledge, Daddy's only hobbies were working and church. He always had two jobs!

I never fully succeeded in this goal of understanding him. Perhaps the years-long gap was simply too large to surmount?

My son, Stevie, moved back to the DC area, and moved in with Daddy for a few years after he left Tuskegee University. The two of them were as "thick as thieves" and got along great. Later, as Daddy's health began to decline, he moved from the DC area out to California, where Janet, Michelle, and I all live. He lived with Janet, but would rotate during the summer between Michelle and I.

Daddy passed away in 2014, a few months shy of his eighty-fourth birthday. Though I never truly felt that I understood him, I can honestly say that Daddy tried! And that is all you can ever ask of anyone.

## TIP #9:

## STAY IN YOUR CHILD'S LIFE

*No matter how difficult the divorce, unless it is court-ordered or something both parents agree to, make an effort to be in your children's life. Divorce is hard on everyone, especially the children, but children are strong and resilient. They will bounce back with time, support, and access to both parents. Do not POOF! Stay in the life of your child. Twenty-plus years is tough to recoup.*

# CHAPTER EIGHT

## 42nd Street and Benning Rd, N.E.

The apartment complex that we lived in, the Benning Heights Apartments, was located up on a hill.

Directly behind the apartments was a wooded area with a path going through them that led down the hill to a large open field area that my new friends and I used to play on. On the corner of 42nd Street and Benning Road was the 42nd Precinct Police station. From time to time, the 42nd Precinct would use the field for various Police Athletic League events, but most of the time it was there for us kids to use.

That would change during the course of one night that I will never forget.

April 5, 1968, *the day after*, began as just an ordinary school day. Ordinary from a student's point of view, except for the emergency staff meeting that was called before school started. The start of the school day seemed ordinary, except the teachers who usually greeted us with smiles were unusually quiet and many had red eyes. Mrs. Wilborn, my third-grade teacher was preparing to give us a test, when the principal came to our classroom and called Mrs. Wilborn outside. I do not know what they discussed, but I remember Mrs. Wilborn coming back into the classroom looking very upset and her eyes were red, as though she had been crying. She told the class to pay attention and listen very carefully as the principal would be making a school-wide announcement on the intercom.

Shortly after her announcement, the principal came on, at first, he sounded rather shaky and his voice trembled a little. He did not at all, sound like the principal we students all feared. He said, *"School is canceled for the rest of the day; you are instructed to go straight home."* I remember that he was very emphatic about us going straight home, so much so that he repeated it. *"Go straight home, do not go to your friend's house, to the store or the library, go straight home."* He further instructed us, *"To check with our parents to determine when school would reopen."*

He ended his announcement by saying, *"God bless you all."*

My classmates and I started to react by cheering that school was letting out early, but Mrs. Wilborn *"shot"* the class a look, so stern, that it would have frozen a polar bear! Now we were really confused, school is letting out early, but no one seems happy. It seems like school might be closed for a while, but why? Are we getting a second Spring Break? If so why, aren't the adults happy and cheerful like they usually are at Spring Break? What is going on? Before dismissing us Mrs. Wilborn again emphasized us going straight home, and if our parents were not at home, we were to stay inside and lock the door. For those who went to a neighbor or relative until our parents returned home, we were told to go to our usual after-care location.

The school was dismissed onto the playground, I met up with Janet and walked down the hill where Riggs Road intersects with South Dakota Avenue to catch the bus home. During our walk I remember asking Janet what was going on, and her saying she didn't know what was going on. In fact, she began to get upset when I kept asking her why she didn't know.

*"You are older than me; you are supposed to know."*

To this Janet angrily said, *"I don't know, so stop bugging me."*

The rest of the walk to the bus stop was done in complete silence. We got on the bus sat down, about five minutes into our ride a passenger boarded the bus highly upset saying, *"They shot Dr. King, they killed Dr.*

*King, we are going to make them pay.*" I looked over to Janet and noticed that she was crying, as was almost everyone on the bus, including the bus driver. The bus driver turned the motor off, opened the doors, and got off. As he got off the bus, he seemed to mutter something to himself. After a few moments he re-boarded the bus, led the entire bus in short prayer, started the bus up again and drove on. As the ride continued, other passengers would board who also expressed their anger at Dr. King being shot. What I did not know was that rioting in response to Dr. King's assassination the previous evening had already started. That was the reason school was closed

Third grade in 1968 was still an age of innocence, so while I had heard the name Rev. Dr. Martin Luther King, and knew somewhat of who he was, and what he was about I did not understand fully. I remember feeling sad on the ride home, but not much more than that. I remember a few years earlier Dr. King speaking in downtown DC by the Lincoln Memorial. I remember my grandparents and many of aunts and uncles coming to our house in Washington the day Dr. King was at the Lincoln Memorial. It wasn't until later that day when my mother explained to me what had happened and why, that I began to cry.

On the news there were reports of rioting, looting, and violence in many cities around the country, including Washington, DC. People were setting fires, burning buildings and stores all along the 8th Street corridor, the Florida Avenue corridor and Georgia Avenue, as well as, other areas around the city. The National Guard was called out to help the police maintain order.

Overnight the field behind our apartment building, the same field that my friends and I played in, became an Army camp. There were large tents, sand bags, jeeps, soldiers, guns, and tanks. Lots of guns!!

My mother made it very clear that I was not to go anywhere near that field while the soldiers remained. When walking down the hill to go to the corner store, I made a point of crossing the street and walking on the sidewalk farthest away from all those tanks. The assassination of

Reverend Doctor Martin Luther King was the fourth major event that occurred in third grade.

Eventually things settled down, the National Guard left, and we kids were able to reclaim our field again. By now Janet and I had lived in our apartment long enough to make a few friends. My two best friends were Michael Pollard who lived in the building next to ours, and Greg Thorne who lived in the apartment complex across the parking lot and in front of our complex. Janet's best friend was a girl named Valerie; I cannot recall her last name. Valerie also lived in the same building as Michael. About four or five blocks from where we lived was the busy intersection of Benning Road and Minnesota Avenue. Near this intersection was a shopping center, a library, and the Senator Movie Theater. Exactly halfway between our apartment complex and this intersection was a funeral home, which is still there today. I believe the name is Sterling Funeral Home.

To get to Benning Road and Minnesota Avenue sometimes we took a shortcut that would bring us behind the Sterling Funeral Home. Other times we would walk south on Benning Road passing directly in front of the funeral home. The opposite side of Benning Road was wooded and was also a place my friends and I would often play.

Growing up, I used to love to watch horror movies, even though they sometimes gave me nightmares. Today I still watch horror movies, only now without the nightmares. I watched all the classics: *Dracula, Frankenstein, The Wolfman, and The Creature from the Black Lagoon.* Zombie movies, on the other hand, were something new to me and quite frightening.

One Saturday Janet and I were home, while my mother was out shopping. Apparently, Janet had gotten permission to go with Valerie to the Senator Theater, the only stipulation was that she had to take me along. *Night of the Living Dead* was the movie that Janet and Valerie had decided upon, along with some other movie that was part of the double feature. When they explained to me what the movie was about... zombies, I really did not want to see the movie.

Remember, if I didn't go with them to the movie, they could not go to the movie. Finally, Janet and Valerie bribed me into going. They promised to buy me a big box of popcorn and a box of candy. Janet and Valerie each had three dollars, so they were feeling generous. So, I said what most, younger brothers would say… okay! On our way to the movies, we took the shortcut that went through the woods behind our apartment complex, through the field, and came out behind the Sterling Funeral Home. We then cut through the shopping center, and crossed the street to the Senator Theater. Janet and Valerie were all excited, as this was one of the first movies they went to alone. They paid for the three tickets, brought me the promised popcorn and candy, as well as their own snacks. I believe they were even talking about going to White Tower after the movie, with the money they had left, to get hamburgers.

Back in my day, the theater would often show a double feature, along with at least one or two cartoons before the movie. From what I recall the showing of fifteen minutes or so of movie previews, that is standard for today, had not yet become practice. We watched the cartoons, and then it was time for the first feature. Usually there was a five-minute delay before the start of the feature movie, this was due to the projectionists having to thread the film through the projector and getting everything set up. During this break, Janet made sure I went to the bathroom.

Finally, the movie started, with *Night of the Living Dead* being the first feature movie. Everything was fine until the part in the movie when the boyfriend spots a "worker" in the cemetery and approaches him to ask some type of question. It has been a while since I have seen the movie, so I cannot recall exactly. The "worker," however, is actually a zombie who starts to attack the boyfriend. Somehow the boyfriend breaks away, and begins to run along with his girlfriend and I think two other friends, to a deserted house on the cemetery grounds. By the time they got to the house, there are zombies everywhere. I had seen enough! I lasted all of five minutes! I was outta there!!

Janet, seeing that I was scared, but not wanting to miss any of the movie herself, told me to go out to the lobby for a few minutes and then come back. I went out the lobby and straight out the front door!

After a few minutes, when I did not come back, Janet went out to the lobby to look for me. When she didn't see me, she asked the ticket taker if he/she had seen me. Apparently, Janet described what I was wearing, because as soon as she did, the ticket taker said, *"Oh yeah I saw that kid. He came tearing out of here like his pants were on fire, and went out the front door!"* Janet went back in to get Valerie, and they both had to leave the theater to look for me. Needless to say, they were not happy!

*Night of the Living Dead* is set during the daytime, not at night like most zombie movies. This particular fact made getting home a problem for me. If zombies could be out during the daytime, they could be out right now! Normally cutting through the woods would have been no problem, but not now, not after having seen five minutes of *Night of the Living Dead*. Going past Sterling Funeral Home, normally, was no big deal, but again not now! For all I knew, zombies were just waiting to get out. Cutting through the shopping center, and going behind Sterling Funeral Home was not an option, because it meant being near the funeral home and then cutting through the woods.

Desperate to get home without being eaten, I did the only thing I could do. I ran up Benning Road past the library, I figured staying near the street was safer than going through or near the woods. As I got one block away from Sterling Funeral Home, I took what I thought was the best course of action. Even though I was running, I did not think passing the sidewalk in front of the funeral home was safe. Directly across from the funeral home on the other side of Benning Road was wooded. So, I chose to run, at top speed, along the dividing line, in the middle of the road! GOD was clearly with me that day, as I am still here to talk about it! I did the same as I ran up the hill of 42$^{nd}$ Street going to our apartment complex. As luck would have it, my mother was back home when I reached our apartment.

I was so out of breath as I was pounding on the door. My mother opened the door saw me, looked around when she didn't see Janet or

61

Valerie, and asked what is going on? All I could say was zombies, quick close the door. I told her what happened, *being careful to leave out the part about me running in the middle of two busy streets.* Eventually Janet and Valerie reached home, and fussed at me for leaving the movie theater. My mother, who had fallen asleep, heard the commotion and came into the living room. She confronted Janet and Valerie and asked what happened. She then turned to me, but before she could say anything, I blurted out, "They made me go; I told them I didn't want to go, but they made me go." My mother sent Valerie home, and Janet got in so much trouble for taking me to see a movie she knew was too scary for me.

It was a long time before Janet would allow me to go with her to the movies again. Years later when I was in high school, I watched *Night of the Living Dead* on TV and wondered what in the world was I so afraid of?

The last major incident that occurred while living at the Benning Heights Apartments involved me inflicting pain upon myself. My friends and I were playing "Throw 'em up, Tackle" in the grassy area, in front of the apartment building, before getting to the parking lot. "Throw 'em up tackle" is a crazy game, involving a football and as many friends as you could find. We usually played this when there were not enough to play a regular game of football. Basically, the football would either be on the ground or someone would throw it up into the air and whoever got the ball would run like crazy through a sea of arms trying to score a touchdown. To see us play this game, and the way we ran around, you would have thought zombies were after us. If you were about to be tackled, you would throw the ball up into the air, someone else would catch it, and then begin to run like crazy. Playing it, was actually a lot of fun.

This particular day we were playing "Throw 'em up tackle." I had the ball and was faking them out like I was in the emergency room. I was running at top speed, before I got corralled. I was about to get tackled and instead of the throwing the ball up in the air, I hung on a second too long. *Wham!* I got tackled hard! What I remember from that hit was how hard it was, and that my entire left side, from the shoulder down was on fire! Now mind you, I was a veteran of several busted heads, a fractured wrist, and a tonsillectomy, but I had never felt pain like this before!

I was helped up by several adults, who had been watching us play. I remember screaming "bloody murder" as they helped me up, and my left arm was hanging down from my left shoulder. I looked like Lurch from Addams Family. I remembered being told that I had not broken my arm, that instead I had dislocated my shoulder. I also remembered discussing whether or not to reset it before taking me to the hospital. Apparently, it was decided by at least three of the men to attempt to reset my shoulder. I was screaming my head off, as two of the men held me still, and Frank, a friend of my mother's, pulled my arm sharply to pop it back into the socket. I can still hear the sharp pop sound, my arm and shoulder made as the joint reconnected. Talk about pain!

A visit to the hospital confirmed no permanent damage, and that I would have to wear a sling for about two weeks. So, the muscles in my shoulder could heal, I was told.

Having experienced fractures and busted heads, I can tell you without exaggeration, a dislocation of a joint is far more painful.

**ZOMBIE MOVIES AND YOUNGER CHILDREN**

*I do not have much to say here, other than zombie movies and younger children are not a good match! On those instances when your oldest child is left in charge, make sure they do not drag your youngest to a movie… they know is too scary… just because they want to see it. Setting ground rules are essential.*

*Even though some ground rules may seem "silly" on the surface, every rule that a parent gives their child is for a reason.*

# CHAPTER NINE

## "Hey, Mister, Wake Up!"

As stated at the outset of this book, I was not a bad kid. I never talked backed or was disrespectful. My mother is Barbadian, or Bajan as we say, so growing up in a West Indian family, talking back or being disrespectful was never really an option.

I was simply mischievous. I could be accused of having a "brain freeze" … long before Slurpee's were invented, on several occasions. This incident was an extreme case of "brain freeze." To this *day* I cannot tell you what I was thinking… or obviously not thinking, when I did what I did.

In Chapter Four, I mentioned how I received the second worst spanking in my life, for attempting to light the bathroom on fire… accidentally. The incident that I am about to share with you in this chapter, was by far the worst spanking I had ever received. I received three spankings, in the same day, from three different people, all for the same offense.

I was born and raised in Washington, DC, but Atlantic City, NJ was my second home. For our family, the Harewoods and Greenidges, Atlantic City was the hub. From there you took I-95 South to DC, Baltimore, MD, Philadelphia, PA, or north to New York City. All but two of my mother's sisters and brothers lived in Atlantic City, plus countless cousins, and of course my grandparents Mom and Pop. Their real names were Edna Harewood and William Harewood, but to us they were simply Mom and Pop.

The Atlantic City that I grew up with was different than the current casino-driven one that exists today. It was a small beach town, with close community among its residents. From my grandparent's house, we could walk three blocks to the boardwalk. I could walk one-half of a block and be at my "Uncle" Joe's house, or walk four blocks and be at my Uncle Granville's or Aunt Elease's house. You get the picture!

My "Uncle" Joe wasn't really my uncle. He was my mother's cousin, but because he was an adult, I could not call him by his first name without some title in front of it. So, he became "Uncle" Joe, and his wife "Aunt" Carolyn. My Uncle Joe had two sons, my cousins, Joseph Jr. (Jo-Jo) and Charles Quentin (Chunky). It is important to note at this time what my Uncle Joe's profession was. He was a mortician and had started his own funeral parlor, Greenidge Funeral Home. Later on, business would expand, and by the time I had finished high school, he had built a larger funeral parlor.

The original Greenidge Funeral Home was a row house with three floors; the funeral parlor was on the ground floor, and the house where Jo-Jo and Chunky lived were the two stories above. There was also a small backyard we could play in. At the opposite end of the block from my grandparent's house, Uncle Joe rented a garage, where he parked the hearse and stored caskets, etc. Uncle Joe made it abundantly clear to myself and all the cousins, that the funeral parlor was no place to play, and that we were not allowed in there unless he or another adult was with us. Here comes the brain freeze!

One morning while visiting at Mom and Pop's, I asked Mom if I could go over to Jo-Jo and Chunky's house. After I was given permission, I walked to the corner of Arctic and New Jersey Avenues, crossed the street and walked the few feet to Uncle Joe's. The screen door was open to the funeral parlor, so I poked my head in and said hello to my Uncle Joe. I asked if Jo-Jo and Chunky were home, he told me they were and that they were upstairs. I closed the door, and went around to the side of the house to climb the bazillion stairs to the upstairs porch, rang the doorbell and then entered. I called out to Aunt Carolyn, it was me, she answered from the kitchen that Jo-Jo and Chunky were upstairs.

We began to play and just hang out, the way three cousins do. At some point, Chunky left with Aunt Carolyn to go somewhere. Jo-Jo and I were left in the house, and with instructions not to bother Uncle Joe, as he had a viewing scheduled later that day and was preparing another body. She also stated she left some sandwiches for us in the kitchen. Having an uncle for a mortician was pretty cool and was always worth a few points when you wanted to gross out a girl. I think I was ten, almost eleven when this incident occurred, old enough to know better is what I was told, as I received my three spankings.

After a while of playing and just hanging out, Jo-Jo and I went down to the kitchen to eat and get something to drink. In the kitchen there was a door that led to a flight of stairs down to the preparation room, where Uncle Joe would prepare the bodies for viewing. For some unknown reason, this door, which was usually closed and locked, was slightly ajar. Jo-Jo and I noticed this and began to discuss: should we or shouldn't we? Should we or shouldn't we? Should we, won out! Jo-Jo and I had been down to the preparation room maybe once before, but never when a body was in there being worked on.

We cracked the door open, and looked down the flight of stairs. We could see that the lights were on, but we could not hear any sound. Still not sure if Uncle Joe was in there working, we snuck down the stairs and peeked around the corner. Nothing! There was no one in there working. A covered body lay on the big table, but there was no one else in there. We got bolder and actually looked around at some of the instruments, making sure we put them back exactly as we found them. There was still no sound. So, we got bolder still, and went into the viewing parlor. There laid out amongst the soft lighting and music was a man in a casket.

For whatever reason, it never occurred to us that this man was dead. On *some* level of consciousness we knew, it just wasn't on the level that we were operating on at that moment. Jo-Jo started first, *"Hey, mister."* Again Jo-Jo said, *"Hey, mister."*

Not wanting to get caught by Uncle Joe, I jumped in by saying, *"Hey, mister,"* *"Hey, mister, wake up."* Jo-Jo and I were experiencing severe brain freeze at this point, because it never popped into our heads that this person, this man, was dead.

I became angered that the man in the casket did not answer us, so I poked him with my finger.

Let me tell you about the human body once we are dead. It becomes among other things very fragile and the skin losses its elasticity. It is only the embalming fluid that gives us any shape, elasticity, and the appearance of life.

So, I poked this man a second time, the third time was the charm. On the third poke, this man lying in a casket sprung a leak. Embalming fluid starting squirting out everywhere. Seeing this Jo-Jo and I did what any self-respecting ten- or eleven-year-old would do, we ran, back upstairs, closed the door, and went up to the third floor to continue playing. Because their house had three floors, there was an intercom system. Sometime later we heard the voice of what sounded like GOD and DEATH all rolled into one. The voice said in angry tone, "Jo-Jo, Stephen, Chunky, and anyone else up there, get down here now!" Chunky by now had returned after being out with Aunt Carolyn. Chunky had no clue what had happened, and Jo-Jo and I were like, *"Do you think he knows?"*

What Jo-Jo and I did not know was that Uncle Joe did indeed know. Shortly after we ran back upstairs, Uncle Joe came back to the funeral parlor. Apparently, he had gone up the street to his storage garage to check on a few things. He came back into the parlor room on his way to continue work on the body we saw laying on the table. He noticed what appeared to be spots on the satin lining of the casket, strange since everything was fine not too long ago. Upon closer inspection, he discovers the body swimming in a pool of embalming fluid.

The viewing for this body was in forty minutes, so he quickly rolls the casket into the prep room, finds the hole made by my finger, sews it up, and re-pumps embalming fluid into the body. He sent an assistant to the storage garage to retrieve another casket, this one more expensive than the one we had damaged. All this was done in about 20-30 minutes. This included drying the suit, the man was wearing. Later I found out that the casket is one of the largest profit centers for a mortician. Because the damage to the casket was not the fault of the deceased man's family, Uncle Joe could not charge them. He simply stated the casket was defective and simply upgraded with a similar casket.

It was only after the viewing that Jo-Jo and I learned of all this frantic activity.

Uncle Joe began his interrogation quite calmly he said:

*"Jo-Jo, Stephen, Chunky, this afternoon I found 'Mr. So and so' in a casket that was full of embalming fluid. Do any of you know anything about it?"*

*"Oh no, Dad, I was playing with Stephen."*

*"Oh no, Uncle Joe, I was playing with Jo-Jo. Weren't we Jo-Jo?"*

Chunky, who really had no clue what was going, said nothing at all.

Again, Uncle Joe continued his questioning, said:

*"It certainly is strange that when I had checked the body ten minutes earlier everything was fine. I also found a hole that looks like it was made by a finger. Are you sure you don't know anything about this?"*

Again Jo-Jo and I lied, and Chunky who was truly innocent was too afraid to say anything in his own defense. We knew Chunky had nothing to do with this, but we were too busy trying to save ourselves, to worry about such minor details as innocence.

Uncle Joe was actually one of my favorite uncles, but not in this instance. I was sure he grew fangs, or claws or something. After our second attempt at lying… no trying to save ourselves… okay lying, his voice got ice cold and became very serious.

*"Last chance, do you want to change your story?"*

He wore all three of us out with his belt! Later, when it was determined that Chunky truly was innocent, he got ice cream. I, on the other hand, got sent home to Mom's house. By the time I had walked the half block, Mom was waiting for me at the front door. I got a second spanking, because of what I did, and because I _made_ Uncle Joe give me a spanking.

*I didn't _make_ Uncle Joe give me a spanking.* He could have given us a pardon. Prisoners on death row receive pardons; we didn't kill anyone, and heck the man was *already* dead.

Later that day, my mother who had been out with my Aunt Gertrude and Aunt Elease came back home. Upon hearing the news, she decided that two spankings were not enough... so she had to get in on the action. I received a third spanking!!

It wasn't until my grandmother's funeral did I touch another dead body... and then just to kiss her.

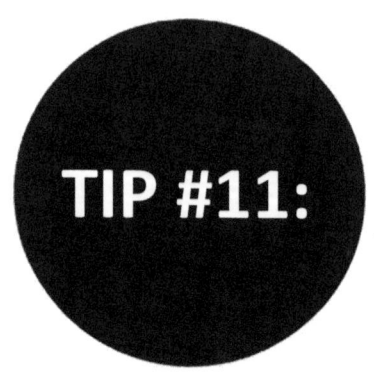

**TIP #11:**

## ONCE REALLY IS ENOUGH

*No real tip here. What can I say, brain freeze of epic proportions!*

*Well, actually, I do have one. If your child has already been punished or spanked by one family member for an incident, there really is no need for additional spankings for the same incident. I can assure you, your child got the message after the first spanking.*

# CHAPTER TEN

## Janet

Janet Lee Franklin is three years older than me, and ten years older than Michelle. As a result, Janet became the de facto "boss" of us whenever Mommy was not home.

It is interesting that even now as adults, our birth order often reigns, more times than not, when settling matters or making decisions. I am quite sure that this is not that unique among families with multiple siblings.

Besides being the oldest, Janet is also the family diplomat. Even to this very day, Janet always tries to make peace between "warring" siblings, family members, cousins… that is just her way. Actually, it is a very admirable trait. I share this to provide some insight into Janet's forceful but diplomatic personality.

As a result of our closeness in age, Janet and I can relate to each other in a manner that often does not need words. Perhaps this is due to the many childhood experiences and challenges that we shared and lived through (I am referring to those experiences apart from me inflicting pain and suffering on myself and the family J). This closeness between Janet and I, is also a source of tension with our younger sister Michelle, though not intentionally. What can I say? Janet and I literally grew up together and had experiences that Michelle simply did not as she had not yet been born.

After we moved to the lower Northeast section of DC, Janet and I continued to attend school in our old neighborhood. Mommy simply felt the schools and teachers were better across town, so Janet and I began a cross-town trek that continued for both of us until we graduated from high school. This is significant, because we were doing this long before "open enrollment" that exists in many school districts today. Prior to that, you attended the school you lived nearby. To get around this, Mommy used the address of a family friend. What this meant for Janet and I, was that being late to school was **NOT** an option, even if we did have to catch two-three city buses. Being late meant going to the Attendance Office. Since Janet was older, the Attendance Office would have spoken with her. A sample conversation if we had ever been late, might have gone something like this:

Attendance: *"So why are you late?"*
Janet: *"It's not my fault, the bus was late."*
Attendance: *"The bus? Why are you catching the bus?"*
Janet: *(Thinking oops!)* *"Um."*
Attendance: *"You only live four blocks away, why are catching a bus?"*
Janet: *"I don't know, ask my mother."*
Attendance: *"Don't worry, we will."*

To avoid all of this drama, the solution was simple, don't be late to school! This put a lot of pressure on the two of us, but somehow, we "bucked up," and were never late. By the time we entered high school, we both were attending private high schools, so being out of boundary was not much of an issue. Just to be sure, we were never late!

The result of being on a tight morning schedule, all those years, has had a profound effect on Janet and I. We tend to be very prompt! Not super early, but prompt. This is in contrast to Mommy. There are different measures of time; there is "CP time" (which usually is an hour after the scheduled start), there is "West Indian time" (which is usually two hours after the scheduled start), and finally there is "Gwen Franklin" time… but I digress.

Our maternal grandmother, Mom, had a "thing" about breakfast. Besides it being the most important meal of the day, it also had to be hot. For adults that is not a problem, for young kids, it could be. Whenever we were in Atlantic City, Mom would get up before everyone else and fix breakfast, the menu varied, but it was always a spread; bacon, eggs, pancakes, waffles (real waffles, not those frozen cardboard ones), fried potatoes, toast, coffee (for the adults only), you name it. The one constant through all of this was porridge!

Mom believed you always had to have a bowl of porridge, no matter what else you had.

Webster's dictionary describes porridge as:

por·ridge

[pôrij]

NOUN

a dish consisting of oatmeal or another meal or cereal boiled in water or milk.

Janet and I were not particularly fans of porridge. Mom had a cabinet over the oven, and in this cabinet, she had every brand of hot cereal known to man. Oatmeal we knew. Mommy served us oatmeal. Mom, had it all, Maypo, Wheatena, Farina, Oatmeal, Cream of Wheat, and at least two or three other brands we had never even heard of. After growing tired of fighting with us to eat in the morning, Mom settled on oatmeal. It was a small win for us, but not enough. Mind you, the breakfast that Mom fixed for us was probably more nutritious. We didn't care, we wanted what our friends ate for breakfast! Our friends back in DC would tell us about eating Frosted Flakes, Fruit Loops, Coco Pops... we had oatmeal!

Janet and I decided to go on a campaign with Mommy. We asked for cold cereal, to which Mommy promptly said NO! I forget how long our campaign lasted, but it was quite a while, maybe a month or two. We would stop for a period of time, and then start up again. One day Mommy came home from the grocery store with a box of Rice Krispies!!

Janet and I saw that box, you would have thought we had won the million-dollar lottery! We were jumping around, whooping it up, all over a box of Rice Krispies! The next morning, we poured the milk on our Rice Krispies, and were just giggling, as we listened to the "Snap, Crackle, and Pop" the cereal made… just like on the commercials.

As time went on, the selection of cold cereals expanded to include; Corn Flakes, Cheerios, and Kix (little rock-hard corn balls, which no amount of milk could soften). We never had sweetened cereals, we didn't care, it wasn't oatmeal. Janet and I were happy, all was well in the kingdom, until Mom found out.

Mom found out that Mommy was giving us a cold breakfast and nearly had a conniption!

The days of Cream of Wheat and Wheatena where over for us. Mom had raised seven children during the Great Depression, so she was not going to be outdone by two grandkids. The test of wills was on! Mom was formidable, after all she was our grandmother, but we had discovered a winning formula… sticking together. After a period of time Mom quietly gave in; she came home from the A & P supermarket, with a box of Nabisco Shredded Wheat. Not the spoon size they have now. No, no—these were the big wheat biscuits that came three to a sleeve. Mom would break them into pieces and pour warm milk over them. That was Mom's concession to us wanting cold cereal.

To this day, every now and then, I will eat spoon-size shredded wheat with warm milk. Maybe it reminds me of Mom… but I have to admit on a cold day it is very warming, tasty, and satisfying.

Janet and I learned the value of sticking together on certain issues. Sometimes it worked, sometimes it didn't.

Mommy had three rules when it came to food.

1) You cannot say you don't like it, if you haven't tried it. Even if you do not like the way something looks, you have to at least try it before you could say you didn't like it.
2) If Mommy wouldn't eat it, then we did not have to eat it (to this day I have never eaten "chitlins" or pig feet… and have no desire to do so).
3) You have to clean your plate!

There are certain dishes that are staples for Bajans; *okra* and *koo-koo* are just two. Janet and I didn't like either!

Mommy would fix okra as part of our dinner and put it on our plate. Janet and I would look at the slimy, running mess that was okra, and were like, "I don't think so" (well actually we thought that, we didn't dare say it). I was known for being a picky and slow eater, for Janet however, this was a new behavior. You have never seen two children pick and eat so slow in all of your life. As *okra* cools, the slime gets thicker, making it even more disgusting. Somehow Janet and I got through the meal. Mommy fixed *okra* a few more times, before she got tired of fussing with us. From that point on, she would fix okra only for herself, another small win for the two of us!

Having fought with us over *okra*, Mommy didn't even bother with *koo-koo*. She already knew! *Koo-koo* is a mixture of cornmeal, onion, and sliced okra, that is mixed into paste and boiled or steamed. The result is a soft but firm pudding like dish. Janet and I were like, no thank you!

As I mentioned, I was known for being a picky and slow eater, Janet not so much, yet Janet also had a few dislikes. One day, at 712 Alabama Ave, S.E., Mommy fixed dinner. Janet complained about not liking peas, I complained about not liking something else. Michelle was probably five when this happened. That was it, Mommy had enough of us ungrateful children, always complaining. She said, *"I am going to the grocery store tomorrow, and whatever I buy will have to last until all three of you apologize to me."* Mind you, Michelle didn't complain about anything, but since there were now three of us, **ALL** of us had to apologize.

The next day came. Mommy went to the Safeway and came home with several bags. I helped bring the bags in as I usually did, partly because I had to, and partly because I always wanted to put the "good stuff" in the front of the cabinets. Janet and I had forgotten about Mommy's threat, that, and there was plenty of "good stuff" now that she had gone to the store. Days went by, the cabinets started getting low. The "good stuff" was getting low or gone. I mean we were down to things like calves' liver (which I could not stand). Even Janet was taking notice about the cabinets, refrigerator and freezer getting low. I think it was Janet who asked Mommy when she was going to the store again. Mommy said, *"I'm not, don't you remember what I said? All three of you have to apologize."*

Janet quickly called a meeting of Michelle and myself. Janet said, *"Mommy is serious, if we do not apologize for complaining, she is not going to Safeway ever again. Mommy said we all have to apologize!"* Reluctantly I agreed, I had no choice, I mean liver, yuck! Michelle on the other hand (mind you she is about five years old said) *"Nope! I didn't do anything. I eat everything Mommy cooks."* Janet and I were shocked. Here is our baby sister telling us, her older siblings, what she is not going to do! I think Janet said something like, *"You have to, I'm your older sister."* Michelle still said, *"Nope, and you can't make me."*

Michelle was the holdout. I think we threatened Michelle saying we were going to tell her scary stories at night so she couldn't sleep. Nothing worked. After a couple of days, Janet came up with the idea of bribing Michelle. I liked the idea, so we pooled together some of our lunch money, and took Michelle down to Leif's market. We let her get whatever she wanted, within our budget of course. She was happy, and that evening at dinner, Janet, Michelle, and I all apologized. The next day the cabinets and freezer were full again!

After that, we were cautious about complaining.

Janet was the oldest, but that didn't mean that Janet was squeaky clean. Janet got into her share of trouble also. Just not as often or as drastically as I did. Janet and Mommy have a great relationship today. They are more like best friends, than Mother and daughter. Growing up, though, in her teenage years, Mommy and Janet used to fight!! Not fistfights, mind you; I mean Janet slamming doors, stomping feet, *"I hate you"* kind of fighting. Basically, over girl stuff.

On those instances when Mommy and Janet were having their shouting matches, I would sit in my room with my door closed… laughing like crazy! Laughing, mind you, without making a sound. I would be sitting on my bed, clutching my belly, and just laughing, bobbing my head as I laughed, all without making a sound! I was laughing because for once, it was not me in trouble! Laughing without making a sound because I didn't want Mommy's anger to shift over to me, *"Oh you think it's funny, let me give you something to laugh about."*

Janet enrolled at Wesleyan University in Middletown, Connecticut, and majored in Biology. See, there is that Franklin-Talbot math and science thing again! For as long as I can remember, Janet had expressed a desire to become either a medical doctor or veterinarian, either way a biology major made sense.

After graduation from Wesleyan, Janet took the MCAT and applied to several medical schools. Her first choice was Georgetown University in our hometown of Washington, DC. The response from several medical schools was not what she expected. Several schools including Georgetown placed her on a waiting list. As a manifestation of her forceful determination, and to keep her options open, Janet also applied to several Public Health programs.

Janet was accepted into the University of Texas at Houston and earned her Masters of Public Health. Shortly after UT, Janet matriculated into Georgetown's Medical School. As if being a full-time medical student was not challenging enough, Janet also became involved with the Student Council. She served as Treasurer, and ultimately President. After graduation from medical school, Janet started a residency at Texas Children's Hospital/Baylor University Hospital in Houston.

Upon completion of her residency, Janet stayed on for a research immunology fellowship. Then she accepted a pediatric hematology/oncology fellowship program position with the National Cancer Institute (part of the National Institute for Health) that also helped to fulfill her Public Health Service requirement from a medical school scholarship she had previously received. Having fulfilled her Public Health Service, Janet was hired by Children's Hospital of Los Angeles / University of Southern California School of Medicine where her specialty of Pediatrics, and her sub-specialty of Hematology/Oncology where in high demand. Janet is now an Executive Medical Director for Clinical Research and Drug Development at a major pharmaceutical company.

I share all of this to point out Janet's determination once she sets her sight on a goal. As her younger brother, I had a front-row seat to all of this. Watching how Janet worked through roadblocks and setbacks helped me develop this same sense of drive.

Janet is a pretty cool sister... I think I'll keep her!!

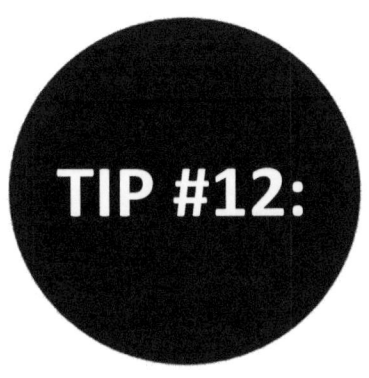

**TIP #12:**

## BE AWARE OF THE COALITION

*This is only applicable when you have two or more children. As parents you hold the upper-hand... most of the time, the exception to this is when your children decide to join forces to resist. Janet and I learned that if we stuck together, we had the potential to "wear" Mommy down. This was our only real tool available to us. It took a while, and mostly we were successful.*

*As parents, you will be able to tell fairly quickly when your children have formed a coalition. Your decision will be how important, to you, is the issue they are resisting, or how do you feel about the campaign they are launching. In other words, choose your battles wisely.*

*On those issues that are less important to you, like cold cereal, feel free to give in... but make them work for it. After all, you are the parent. On those issues that are non-negotiable, like being grateful, hold your ground. Instead of them wearing you down, you wear them down.*

# CHAPTER ELEVEN

## 712 Alabama Avenue, S.E.

I cannot recall if we moved to 712 Alabama Ave. while I was still in the sixth grade, or if we moved during the summer just before I was to begin junior high school. Either way, some of my more memorable moments occurred while living here.

712 Alabama Ave. was to be home for me until I graduated from High school and began college. By the time we moved I had a new baby sister, her name was Michelle. Michelle was ten years younger than me, so as the second oldest she largely became my responsibility whenever Janet or our mother was not home. As her big brother, I alternately took turns being her tormentor and protector. According to Michelle, I was more of a tormentor!

712 Alabama Ave. was in a part of Southeast DC known as Congress Heights; it was supposed to be a really tough part of town. I say supposed to be, because I never got that sense of the area. It was simply home! My friends and I knew to stay away from certain streets; or that when you walked down the hill to the public swimming pool by Valley Green you always walked in a pack. I mean sure we knew basic street survival, but overall, I never felt like danger was lurking around each corner.

The three-to-four-block area around my house became the site for most of my adventures, and was where most of my friends lived. Occasionally we would venture out of our immediate neighborhood to go to the pool, library, movies, or when we were sent to the grocery store. To give you a sense of geography, the block that I lived on comprised Alabama Ave. at one end, 7th and 8th streets on both sides, and Portland Street at the other end. The alley that joined this block looked like a capital *I*, with our backyard being directly at the intersection on the long part of the *I* with one of its feet. I also had friends who lived on 9th street.

It is important to note that near our house was St. Elizabeth's Mental Hospital, or "St. E's" as it was called in the neighborhood. "St. E's" was quite a large facility and was run by the DC government. If you were in your car driving East on Alabama Ave. it would take you approximately three minutes before you completely passed the grounds of "St. E's." By the same token, driving along Martin Luther King Blvd. it would take approximately five minutes, with St. E's taking over both sides of the street once you passed the Safeway grocery store, before you completely passed its grounds. "St. E's" was bordered by a huge wrought-iron fence, with a portion of it wrapping around my neighborhood where 8th Street and Portland Street each came to an end. It was here that a huge gap existed in the wrought iron fencing. How it got there I don't know; it was there long before I moved into the neighborhood, but it was through this gap that my friends and I spent countless hours playing football and for a short time baseball.

Why you ask, because "St. E's" had vast green grassy areas that was perfect for our football dreams. To my friends and I, this was our personal R.F.K. Stadium. We also played football in various backyards, and of course we played touch football in the alley, but the preferred location was "St. E's." Of course, we had to watch out for the guard patrols, and would scatter when they came around. We would wait awhile and then return to continue our game. Of course, this gap in the fence worked both ways, and every once in a while, a "crazy" person would escape through the fence. During these moments, my friends and I would sit on the porch of one of the guys who lived along Portland Street to watch the excitement, as the person was "recaptured."

We would stay near the front door of whose ever house, just in case the "crazy" person got too "crazy"! Mostly they were harmless.

As an adult, I later learned that the side of "St. E's" near us housed individuals who were developmentally delayed. The truly dangerous or criminal individuals were housed on the other side of MLK Blvd. behind the huge stone walls that you would see as you drove along.

Despite the occasional "escapes" by residents, and us "breaking in," the gap in the wrought-iron fence strangely enough was never closed up. I think there was an unwritten agreement, as long as we didn't damage anything or bother anyone; we could play on the grounds. I can tell you we had many fun times playing there. I will come back to this later.

Moving into a new neighborhood meant making new friends, which proved to be very easy as there were many boys my age in the area. My closest friends were Robbie (Robert Howard Jr.), Greg (Greg Thorne) who had lived near me when I lived at the Benning Heights Apartments, Greg Lampley, whom we all called "G2," and the only white guys on the block Dave and Steve Dinkel (for reasons unknown we called Steve "Teat"). These were the guys I hung with mostly, and with whom I had most of my adventures.

There were others also like Calvin ("KK") who lived on 9th Street, "Kippy" (I cannot recall his real name) and his brother Donald who lived next door to me, and two brothers whose names I cannot recall, they lived on the other side of Robbie's house. There were a few girls who were part of our circle; Madeline and Katrina (the sister of "Kippy" and Donald) were tomboyish and good at football and basketball. As they began to develop, they didn't seem to mind when we "accidentally" would grab a feel while guarding them or tackling them. There are a few other guys whose faces I can see, but I cannot recall their names.

Robbie's family and mine became very close and for a while were almost like one large family. Robbie had a sister named Cheryl, she and my sister Michelle, who were around the same age, became close friends. Later, as they got older, they would be sent on reconnaissance missions by our parents to find us, when it was time for dinner or when we were going out. Finding us really wasn't hard because our parents pretty much knew where we were. It was, however, just out of shouting distance. Greg had a younger brother named Brian and a sister named Linda. Brian initially was annoying, but later turned out to be quite cool. Linda was the first girl I had a crush on. This was largely due to the fact that Linda had developed faster than other girls in the block, I was always finding some reason to brush against her or sneak a feel. On a few occasions she actually allowed me to grab a solid feel, although she never let me actually see them.

Growing up during this time; was like one long adventure. During the school week because of my daily cross city treks, I didn't get outside much. The weekends, however, were another story. I practically lived outside! A typical Saturday comprised of; waking up, cleaning up in the bathroom, eating breakfast, doing your chores and then boom out the door! It was usually around 11:00 a.m. before enough of us had finished our morning chores and gathered to decide what the day's plan was. We would hang out for the day until it was time for us to go in, which for all us was the same universal curfew. We had to be in the house by the time the streetlight came on! I will come back to this later.

Money was a scarce commodity, though we always seemed to have what we needed, our parents didn't have that much extra to give us. Our first goal was usually to gather empty soda bottles, seven- or ten-ounce ones were worth 5 cents, and 16-ounce ones were worth 10 cents. We would wash them out (clean bottles were worth 1–2 cents more), and take them down to the corner store, Leif's. There we would cash them in and buy our stash for the day; Now & Laters, Squirrel Nuts Zippers, Mary Janes, Chick-o-Sticks, shoestring licorice, Lemonheads, Boston Baked Beans, Atomic Warheads, Tastykakes, and of course Rock Creek sodas. Many times we would pool our money and get bigger items like a sub or some dill pickles.

The owner of the store Leif would store the bottles outside in a fenced-in area, waiting for them to be picked up, except for one crate that always sat outside of this fenced area. Whenever we were short by a bottle or two, we would sneak around to this unguarded crate of bottles and take one or two. So that it wasn't too obvious, we would dirty them up a little and sacrifice the extra 1–2 cents, and turn them in. We used to think we were being slick. It wasn't until years later that I realized what Leif was actually doing by placing the one unguarded crate outside for our access.

On other occasions we would go around and do small jobs to get extra money. At the time we were just doing what came naturally, looking back now I realize that we were all learning life lessons about the value of money and working for something you want.

For whatever reason, the neighborhood that I lived in had a wealth of fruit trees and vines, just ripe for the picking… so we did! My backyard had a peach tree, Mr. Davis who lived in the other house like ours, had a plum tree, there were at least two apple trees in other yards, and some old lady who had a grapevine. Needless to say, when we short on money, which was quite often, we would raid the various fruit "stores" in the neighborhood. Mr. Davis, who was quite mean, got tired of us raiding his plum tree, so he put a very high fence (maybe 10 feet) all around his yard. This didn't stop us. We became very good at quickly climbing the fence, jumping down into the yard, and scaling the fence again before he could come outside. It was always a challenge not to get caught!

Most of our fun was self-made, and we became very industrious at building things; skateboards, basketball backboards to mount on telephone poles, etc. Torturing bugs, and girls were always good for fun. Because of an incident when I was younger, I was scared of bees… I still am. I am not allergic to them; I just had a really bad experience with them.

My friends knew this, so often times torturing bugs also meant torturing me as well. One of our favorite things to do was to get an empty mayonnaise jar, wash it out, and then pour a little ammonia in the jar. We would shake the jar up real good and then pour out the ammonia, with the vapors still inside. We would then catch large bumblebees in this same jar. After a few moments we would dump the bumblebees out on the ground and watch them stumble around until the effects of the ammonia vapors wore off and they flew off. Other times we would catch yellow jackets or "yellow jacks" as we called them in jars with air holes punched in them. The task here was really to watch me freak out! Upon catching several "yellow jacks" they would shake the jar to get them angry and then put the jar close to my ear so I could hear the angry buzz. My friends always thought it was funny to see my reaction, I never thought it was funny.

Growing up in DC my friends and I played mostly football and basketball, because there was no professional baseball team that we could identify with. The Washington Senators left to become the Texas Rangers. Baltimore had the Orioles, but then as now there was a rivalry between DC and Baltimore, so rooting for the Orioles, at least in public was not permitted. Depending upon the size of our group for the day, determined if we played touch or tackle football, and where we played. Touch football was usually played in the long part of the "I" in our alley. Occasionally we would play it where Portland Street dead-ended into the "St. E's" fence. For tackle football we had several choices, Robbie's backyard, an abandoned house at the corner of 8th Street and Portland Street, that had a large grass area bounded by bushes, and or course our favorite "St. E's." Robbie had the largest backyard of all of us, and his mom was really cool, serving us sandwiches, drinks, and homemade donuts.

I mentioned how Robbie's family and mine were very close. Often times I would be over at Robbie's around dinner time and would ask to stay if they were having something that I really liked. Robbie would do the same if he was at my house, calling home to compare what was for dinner. Robbie's father took me under his wing, and would often take me with him, when he and Robbie were doing father and son things. I knew our families were close, however, I did not know how close until this one incident.

Robbie, myself, and the guys were playing tackle football one summer day at "St. E's" when it started to rain. In Washington, DC rain is nothing new, as it rains frequently, especially during the summer with frequent thunder and lightning storms. As the rain became heavier and the thunder began, we thought about ending the game… but only for a moment! After all we reasoned, the Redskins don't stop playing when it rains, and since we were playing in our personal R.F.K. Stadium the game went on. Playing in the rain took on a whole new dimension whenever we tackled someone, water would spray out in front of you as you slid in the grass. Faking people out as you ran with the ball would often result in you wiping out on the slick grass, and passing the ball came to a stop as it was too heavy and slick to grab properly. By the end of the game, we all looked like we had been in two or three wars. Whatever had been white was now beyond being muddy, it was now some weird shade of gray.

Tired and worn out, but laughing as we recounted our exploits in the rain, we walked down the alley. Our shoes and socks were so waterlogged that we squished as we walked. Shirts were hanging down, stretched out of shape and also waterlogged. We dropped off Dave and "Teat" at the north end of the alley before turning to head down the long part of the "I." Robbie and Greg lived side by side a few feet from where my backyard intersected the alley. Robbie went in first while Greg and I talked for a few moments longer, in the rain. Unknown to me Robbie's mother had called my mother upon seeing Robbie as he entered the backdoor:

*"Gwen, this is Jackie, whatever you do, do not let Stephen in the house."*
*"Go to the back door and you will see what I am talking about."*

My mother met me as I was about to reach for the doorknob. She took one look at me, and told me to strip! I was shocked because I said what? My mother said you heard me strip… you are not coming in this house looking like that! Tracking dirt and mud everywhere, you must have lost your mind, now strip! I protested again saying, but the guys will see me, even though no one else was outside because… it was raining!

My mother made me, her only son, strip down to his underwear, which was now also a weird shade of gray, outside in the pouring rain, before she allowed me to set foot in the house. Once in the house she told me to head straight for the tub and take a bath, and wash my hair. As the tub later emptied, I was amazed at how much dirt and grass there was. Did all of that come off me? Of course, the answer was YES!!

As I mentioned earlier, my friends and I all had the same basic curfew. We had to be in the house by the time the streetlights came on. On special occasions like neighborhood cookouts, we just had to be in the yard where the cookout was being held by the time the streetlights came on. Anyone who grew up during this time period can relate to being home by the time the streetlights came on, and knows that from that first hum or crackle there really was not much time before the light was up full.

For my friends and me, this was always a challenge. We could be playing basketball in the alley over on 9th Street, with our homemade backboard decorated with our favorite teams. As soon as we heard that first hum or crackle, the game was over!! It was an unspoken rule that whoever had the ball at that moment took it home until tomorrow. This was crucial, because there was not enough time to figure out whose ball it was, we ALL had to be somewhere… *fast!!* To see us scatter was a sight to behold, it was like seeing roaches scatter when you turn on the light, I mean we were gone!!

All of us were running at "top speed," dashing across streets without looking, taking shortcuts, racing down the alley! How we managed to get home with none of us getting hit by a car, or hurt I will never know. Somehow, though, we managed this feat for many a year, and not once did any of us get injured or maimed.

GOD truly does look out for babies and fools!

When we were not playing games, or racing home before the streetlight came up full, we had another problem to contend with. The house on the corner of Alabama Ave. and 7th Street

Just like on ancient maps that said, "Here there be dragons" for unexplored areas, this house should have had a sign that said, "Here there be Dobermans!"

The house on the corner of Alabama Ave. and 7th Street was across the alley from Greg Thorne's house, and next door to G2's house. The house was a large white house that sat in the middle of fairly large yard, with a ridiculously low white picket fence, on three sides. The side next to G2's house had a higher-than-normal chain-link fence. In addition to the fence being low, it was also bent down in many areas courtesy of the Doberman Pincers jumping at and over it.

There were two calls that more than anything got everyone's attention.

*"Dobermans out!"*

This meant that the six to seven Dobermans that lived at this house were out in the yard. As long as no one went down that part of the alley (as if we were crazy), usually there was no problem. Until some unwitting fool walked past the yard, causing the Dobermans to rush the fence!

*"Dobermans loose!"*

This was the call we all dreaded. That meant that usually one to two Dobermans had jumped the fence, and where OUT!!! If we were in the part of the alley near my house, which meant you could look down the alley and actually see the Dobermans everyone scattered. We climbed fences, got on the roof of Greg's garage, or went inside until the Dobermans were caught.

I can't tell you how the system worked, or who did the scouting, but it worked nonetheless.

One day Robbie, Greg Thorne, and I were sitting on Greg's front porch on 7th Street. We were just talking, kicking back, when I think Greg said to Robbie; "Hey, isn't that your dad?" Why is he running? So, we all jumped up and climbed the rail of Greg's porch to get a better view. There was Robbie's dad in a full-out run, arms pumping and everything, and then we saw the reason why he was running... perhaps seven to ten yards behind him and closing, also running at top speed, was one of the Dobermans!

Apparently, the Doberman had gotten out earlier, with no one being aware. By now we are all frantic, especially Robbie. We all yelled to Robbie's dad, *"run, Mr. Howard, run!!"* Robbie's dad reached the fence that surrounds their yard, and did something I had never seen before or again since. He vaulted the fence in one leap and ran into the backyard, closing the gate to the ten-foot wooden privacy fence that separated the front yard from the back.

The Doberman, upset it had lost its meal, stood there barking and growling. Before walking past Greg's front gate, and then hopping back into its yard. To put the vault that Robbie's Dad performed into

90

perspective, allow me to describe the fence that surrounded both Robbie's and Greg's yard.

The fence first comprised a stone wall, perhaps three-four feet high. Many times, we would just sit on this portion of the fence just talking. On top of this stone wall, slightly set back, there was your standard chain-link fence, I am not sure of the height of the chain-link portion, other than it was the same height that a chain-link fence would be by itself. To see Robbie's father, reach up and grab the *top* of the *chain-link fence,* and then vault over the entire structure in one leap was absolutely amazing!! Needless to say, Robbie's father earned many cool points with us behind this, and was the talk amongst us whenever things got slow and we had nothing else to talk about.

Humans: 1

Dobermans: 0

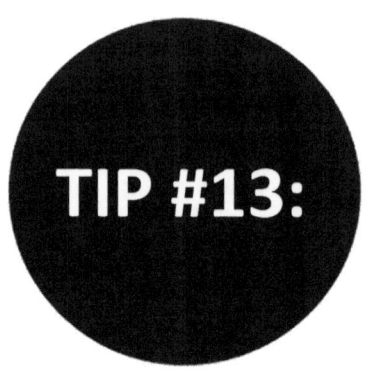

TIP #13:

## TRUST ME, YOU REALLY
## DON'T WANT TO KNOW

*To put it simply, if your child comes into the house, flustered, out of breath, telling you how great you are, and just overall happy to see you.*

*Your child just did something incredibly stupid and almost killed or maimed themselves. Racing home to beat a curfew and crossing busy streets without looking qualifies!*

*Don't fret over it, don't waste time running an inquisition. Trust me… you really don't want to know! In due time… your child will tell on themselves!*

# CHAPTER TWELVE

## "We Didn't Mean for it to Land in the Back Seat"

As I mentioned in the previous chapters, much of our fun was self-made. Nintendo and Xbox were decades away from being invented. For my friends and I, the ultimate form of punishment was to be grounded and not be allowed to go outside.

As my friends and I would go around to each other's homes, we always walked away gloomy when we were told by whoever's mother, that so and so was on punishment. We would always walk away thinking what did he do to deserve such a harsh punishment. At the same time, we hoped it wasn't catching, as if being on punishment was the flu or some other illness.

Being grounded was worse than the death penalty in our eyes, I mean not being able to go outside… didn't that qualify under cruel and unusual punishment? Now a days, telling a child that he or she _has_ to go outside, that they _can't_ stay inside and play Nintendo or Xbox… _that is_ the punishment. I can attest to the cruel and unusual aspect of being grounded, as I experienced more than my share of groundings! Back during this time, being grounded meant being confined to your room, no TV, no anything, other than what was in your room. It was during these many confinements that I developed a love of reading.

My eighth through tenth grade years of school were eventful. Not for what happened at school, but rather for what happened at home during these years. Even though I am not built for playing competitive football, that never stopped my dreams of being the next Larry Brown or

Charley Taylor (former Washington Redskins star players). In basketball I dreamed of being the next Lew Alcindor (his name before he changed it to Kareem Abdul Jabbar) or Mike Riordan or Kevin Porter (former Washington Bullets star players). In fact, the hook shot, long before it became the sky hook, was my favorite shot.

Around this time Nike and Adidas came on the scene. Before them all you had were Chuck Taylor's or Jack Purcell "Blue Tips." Of course, there were Keds and P.F. Flyers, but they were viewed as being for little kids. Chuck Taylor's only came in two colors, white or black, high tops or low tops. If you wanted color, you had to add color shoe laces. Robbie and I were the first two guys on the block to have either Nikes or Adidas. Robbie had a pair of blue suede Nikes, and I had a pair of red suede Adidas. Let me tell you about those red suede Adidas. First of all, why red suede Adidas you ask? Simple, my favorite player on the NBA's Washington Bullets, Mike Riordan, wore red suede Adidas. Kevin Porter, Robbie's favorite player on the Bullets, wore blue suede Nikes.

It took me a full year of campaigning and asking multiple people in my family before I got them. Largely because of the cost. In the early 1970s these red suede Adidas cost $25.00, which back then was a LOT of money for *play* shoes! Back then your parents could buy you an entire outfit; shirt, pants, socks, underwear *and* shoes for that amount of money. I first asked my mother who promptly laughed at me; I then asked my grandfather "Pop" who also thought I was crazy, and in his Bajan accent began to tell me how he was not made of money, etc. My Uncle Bill, who was also my godfather, became my next target. He never actually told me no, he just used the universal, "I will think about it." So, for the rest of the year whenever I saw him or spoke to him on the telephone I would ask, "Have you thought about it yet?"

Finally, I wore him down. After one full year of working, campaigning... begging... I got my red suede Adidas! I wore those shoes with so much pride. I wore them until the red dye was just a memory, and my shoes were faded gray with just a hint of red.

I was in the eighth grade still holding on to my football dreams, when something happened that forever changed and ultimately ended this dream. Robbie, Greg, G2, and I were playing tackle football in

Robbie's backyard, in the long portion of his yard. Robbie, Greg, and I had even formed our own team, complete with football helmets that we painted… strangely enough to resemble the Toronto Argonauts of the Canadian Football League. So here we are wearing our helmets, G2's helmet didn't match, but that was okay, we were playing football. Greg and I were on one team, while Robbie and G2 were on the other team. Greg and I had just scored a touchdown and were throwing off, our version of a kick-off. Robbie caught the ball with G2 blocking and started to run the ball back. I was drawing a bead on Robbie when G2 caught me with a vicious roll block! Vicious not in that it was illegal, or dirty, vicious in the sense that I did not see it coming and that it was so well executed. The roll block pinned my left arm to the ground, unfortunately the rest of my body kept going!

The sound my arm made as it broke was loud and crisp, and sounded very much like a dry branch snapping. It brought the entire game to a screeching halt. That plus the fact that I was screaming! Robbie and Greg ran to get Robbie's mom, while G2 kept apologizing saying he didn't mean it. I knew he didn't mean it and I let him know that, in the meantime, my arm was a mess. Robbie's mom came outside, and with the help of the guys got me to sit up while clutching my arm. While Robbie, G2 and myself held my arm, Greg and Robbie's mother helped me to my feet and inside Robbie's house.

Robbie's mother called my mother frantic! She was a rookie to the "Stephen experience!" My mother being the savvy veteran that she was, calmed Robbie's mom, and told her:

*"She would be over as soon as she finished washing Michelle's hair."*

My mother walked across the alley about fifteen minutes later. By this time Robbie's mom had taken a pillow case, and had made a sling for my arm to rest in. Robbie, Greg, and G2 had gone into Robbie's room and were playing while I waited for my mother. Robbie's mom was apologizing for the accident and my mother was like:

*"Jackie, girl, don't even worry about it. This boy has been accident-prone all his life, don't even lose sleep over it."*

My mother took me to Cafritz Hospital down the hill—now it is called Greater Southeast Community Hospital. They x-rayed my arm and confirmed what my mother and I already knew… it was broken.

My arm was set, placed in a plaster cast and I was sent home. Strangely enough, breaking my arm while playing football, was like a badge of honor around the neighborhood, it signified toughness… or something. G2 earned cool points also, for throwing the block that broke my arm. The doctor at the hospital before sending me home told me to be careful and not to do anything to crack my cast… why did he tell me that?

Didn't he know that as soon as you tell a fourteen-year-old *NOT* to do something that is *EXACTLY WHAT THEY DO!*

I blame that doctor at Cafritz Hospital for what happened next. Had he not put the idea in my head, it never would have happened… well, it probably would not have happened… maybe not so soon! I think it took me about two weeks to crack my cast while playing touch football (I wasn't totally crazy) in the alley. Of course, it was about another week or so before this was officially discovered during a follow-up visit to Dr. Nasser's office (yes, I remember his name). I emphasize the official discovery because I was well aware of it long before that time. The throbbing caused by the bones shifting was my first clue. Of course, I did not dare tell my mother, she would have killed me! When Dr. Nasser shared his discovery with my mother, she of course was surprised. When she looked at me with a questioning look, I simply said with a straight a face as I could, *"I don't know what happened; it just cracked."*

Since the school year was almost over, Dr. Nasser waited until the summer before addressing the resetting of my arm. This began a three-year ordeal that forever ended my dreams of football glory. As soon as the school year ended, Dr. Nasser scheduled the procedure, which required my being hospitalized in order to break and reset my arm. The day of the procedure was uneventful, with me being sedated and put to sleep while my arm was re-broken, and then reset properly. I woke up in my hospital bed with a brand-new white plaster cast on my left arm.

I spent the entire summer in a white plaster cast under the careful watch of my mother and grandparents alternately. I couldn't do anything! When the cast came off just before the start of the ninth grade, even without me cracking my cast, the bones had shifted. The result is that I appeared to have three elbows, not one. Dr. Nasser discussed with my mother various options. My misaligned arm was not life-threatening, but if not addressed it could result in stunted growth of that arm. Since

I am left-handed, my mother wanted to hold off as long as possible so as not to interfere with school. It was decided over Easter Break (at this time it was still called Easter Break, before being politically correct came into being) to perform the operation.

The operation on my left elbow was extensive and included the re-aligning/ recreation of my elbow joint and involved the moving of nerves to facilitate proper alignment. I woke from surgery to find two pins sticking out through my cast, with two screws and wire holding my elbow together under the cast. With the pins sticking out, any kind of bump was painful. Needless to say, I was very careful, without having to be told to do so. By the time the cast, screw and pins came out, Dr. Nasser had moved into a newly built office building. Looking back on it now, I wonder why a floor wasn't named in my honor, or at least a room, after all I am sure my mishap helped pay for at least a portion of that building.

It was not until my junior year of high school that I started to wear short sleeve shirts again, due to the embarrassment of the scare left on my arm. In the dead of summer, I was wearing buttoned long-sleeve shirts. Even when I began to wear short sleeves, I wore long short-sleeve shirts that covered my elbow. I also developed a completely fabricated story involving me being the "filling" in a vicious three-way sandwich-type hit. In my version, which was first unveiled when I started college, I played for my high school football team and was laid out by a hard hit, involving a linebacker, safety, and cornerback all hitting me simultaneously. I kept the hardware that came out of my arm, in a small glass jar, and proudly showed off the pins, screws, wire and a piece of flesh that had dried in the wire. As well as I told that story... none of it had actually happened. It simply sounded better than saying I was the victim of a well-executed roll block, while playing backyard football.

Looking back now, it is amazing to me that I did not become a potato chip magnate or something. During my ninth grade (in between surgeries) and tenth grade years, I had this fascination with trying to create the perfect potato chip. I would take potatoes and experiment with slicing them to different thickness, with or without skin, and then frying them in oil.

One day I was home alone with my sister Michelle. Michelle, who was four at the time, insists her version is true. What I am relating is what I recall, and am confident my version is more accurate. Michelle swears I was making home-made donuts when the burned-hair incident occurred. Actually, it was a few years later that my focus shifted from potato chips to donuts.

I was in the kitchen working on my perfect potato chip, when Michelle came into the kitchen. She asked me what I was doing, and asked a series of "why" questions. To quiet her I asked her if she wanted to help me. To which she said yes. I just started a fresh batch of potato chips, and was watching them in the oil when I picked up Michelle and told her how to carefully use the spatula to turn them over. Michelle has always had long hair, and on this day her hair was done into two long braids on either side of her face. The stove was gas… you can imagine what happened next.

As I was holding Michelle up so she could flip the chips, she leaned forward and one of her braids caught fire. Thankfully Michelle was blissfully unaware as she was intent on flipping the potato chips. I on the other hand was very much aware, and was trying to put out her burning hair, without dropping her into the hot oil, or have myself catch fire. Of course, by now Michelle was aware what was happening, but *thankfully* she did not squirm in my grasp. Had she squirmed, this story would take on an entirely different tone… largely because I would have been dead, and therefore unable to tell it. Somehow, I managed to put out her hair without getting either one of us further injured.

Now I am absolutely convinced that GOD does indeed look out for babies and fools!

Now that the immediate danger is over, I was trying to think what to tell my mother. I was also busy bribing Michelle to be quiet and stop crying. Have you ever smelled burnt hair…?

Doing the only thing I could think of… at the time, I told Michelle to put on one of her knitted hats and not tell anyone. Of course, sometime later my mother came home, noticed Michelle wearing her knitted hat inside the house… thinking it strange she asked Michelle why she was wearing it. With all the seriousness that a four-year-old can muster, Michelle told our mother; *"Stephen said to not tell anyone."* Michelle took off her knit hat, and revealed the burned mess that was the right side of her hair.

I was upstairs in my room and had lost track of where Michelle was. My plan was to walk Michelle into my mother's room and tell her how I had saved Michelle's life, leaving out the part about me holding her over the lit stove. By the time I heard my mother call, *"Stephen Louis Franklin!"* I knew that story was not going to work! I think I was grounded for about two weeks behind that incident.

I think that episode scared me for life, and that is why I am not the potato chip magnate… that I should be!

I mentioned earlier about all the fruit trees in our neighborhood. It was during one summer day before my tenth-grade year, when Greg, Robbie, and I were bored. It was during July, so firecrackers were plentiful, even though we were not supposed to have them. I cannot recall whose idea it was, probably a communal one, to take some of the partially ripe peaches off my tree and blow them up with firecrackers.

It started off simply enough with the three of us digging out a hole using a stick, placing a firecracker inside, timing the fuse and then throw them up and watch them explode. After a few of these explosions, we took it a step further. We gathered a bunch of peaches and climbed onto Greg's roof, largely because Greg's father wasn't home. From there we started throwing peach bombs out over 7th Street and watch them explode. Who could have foreseen what was about to happen… probably anyone and everyone… *except us!* As luck would have it, a taxicab was driving along down 7th Street heading towards Alabama Ave.

Greg who was the strongest of us three had just finished throwing a peach bomb into the air as this taxicab happened along. Because it was summer, the taxicab had its windows down. The three of us watched in horror as Greg's peach bomb flew into the rear driver's side window of this taxicab. Realizing what was about to happen, we tried to watch *and* hide at the same time. Greg who was real good at timing fuses must have put a long timer on the fuse, because it seemed like forever before we heard "boom"! Simultaneously the taxicab swerved up onto the sidewalk crashing into a bush! Greg, Robbie, and I got as flat as is humanly possible on that roof. You have never seen three teenagers trying so hard to become *one with the roof… "see the roof, be the roof"* … trust me we were trying to *be* the roof. We could only hear the curses coming from the mouth of the taxicab driver as he screamed and yelled at his unseen attackers, we did not dare squirm or move for fear of giving our position away.

Fortunately for us, the way Greg's roof was pitched the driver could not see us. After the driver stopped screaming and cursing, he finally checked his taxicab for damage. Since there was no damage, *we knew* because the driver screamed this out to the air and his unseen attackers, he backed off the sidewalk and left. The three of us stayed on Greg's roof as flat as possible for another thirty minutes, just to make sure the driver didn't circle around the block and come down the alley from behind us.

For some reason (called self-preservation) I never told my mother about this incident… that is until now! In fact, there are probably several incidents that I never told my mother!

Like I said before, I was not a bad kid just mischievous. We did not mean for it to land in the back seat… it just did!

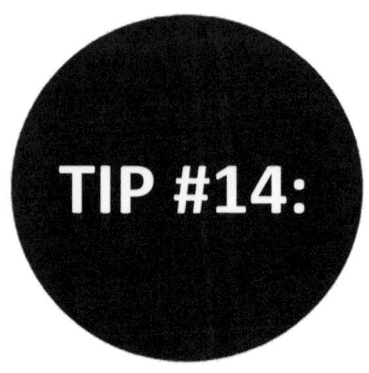

**TIP #14:**

## BE PATIENT, LET YOUR CHILDREN TELL ON THEMSELVES

*Your accident-prone child will invariably engage in all manner of escapades, many of which will not be well thought out. Case in point, my friends and I throwing "peach bombs" out over a busy street. Some of these escapades you will know about in a timely manner, for any number of reasons; they got caught while doing it, a neighbor report, or self-inflicted injury.*

*Even with all these "reporting" mechanisms, invariably there will be incidents that you simply will not know about. Unless your child tells on themselves! My mother was the master at this. I would get in trouble for something, and my mother, the veteran of Stephen mishaps, would use the ultimate line on me. She would say, "Now, you know why you're in trouble, don't you?"*

*Of course, I am expected to respond and acknowledge my misdeed. My mother, would be patient and wait because she knew I was about to tell on myself. With my mother waiting, I am going through my mental rolodex, trying to gauge what she probably knew about. Invariably, I would fail and confess to some incident that she was NOT aware of.*

*My mother would then say; "Oh, I wasn't aware of that one, but since you owned up to it, we will just add it onto…" and then she would tell me what I was actually in trouble for.*

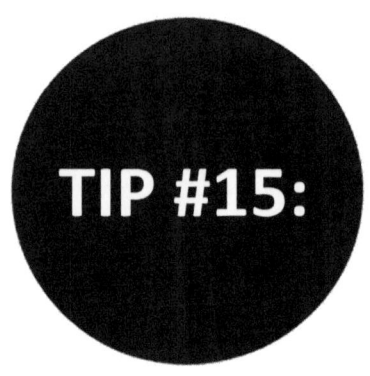

# TIP #15:

## CHECK THE CAST OFTEN

*The minute you tell a child what not to do, that immediately becomes the thing they want to do. This is magnified with an accident-prone teenager. My doctor telling me to be careful and not crack my cast, pretty much assured I was going to crack my cast.*

*Casts nowadays are made from fiberglass and are more durable than the plaster casts of my day. Nonetheless, fiberglass cast can also crack. A cast "wellness check" from time to time might be in order.*

# CHAPTER THIRTEEN

## Michelle

Michelle Lisa Franklin is the youngest of us three. That basic fact never really stopped Michelle from acting like she was older. Having two siblings that are ten and thirteen years older than you, respectively, I guess makes you feel and act older. I guess??

For the purposes of this story, the age gap between Michelle and I presented challenges. As this story relates the first eighteen years of my life, Michelle was only around for the last eight of those years. A ten-year age difference is pretty significant among children, not so much among adults.

The difference between fifteen and five is huge, the difference between fifty and forty, not so much!

I did not consult my sister Michelle, or anyone else for that matter, regarding their specific chapters. I did, however, let each person review their chapter upon completion. Getting their perspective on events so long ago, was helpful.

For those with younger siblings, beware, even when you think they are not watching you, they are!! That is what younger siblings do.

As for acting older, both Mommy and our grandmother "Mom" often said Michelle had "an old soul." They would point to her often saying or talking about things you would not expect from someone her age. Our grandmother, Mom, and Michelle shared the same birthday, November 12th, and as a result they were especially close. Alternately,

Mom would often talk about Michelle "being here before," because she would say or know things beyond her age.

In reality much of saying and knowing things, stemmed from her listening and observing Janet and me. Now that we are all adults, Michelle will often comment, I watched what you two did and learned what not to do!

When Michelle was little, everyone in the family called her Mickey. Mom even made up a little song calling her "Mickey, Mickey, Bamboo!"

By the time I turned fifteen, our older sister Janet was beginning her freshman year at Wesleyan University in Connecticut. This meant the duties of babysitter fell on me when Mommy was not home. As mentioned earlier, my role ranged from protector to tormentor. I freely admit when Michelle got "on my nerves" I became her tormentor. Of course, later on I get in trouble with Mommy, but at the time...

One time that stands out when I was acting as Michelle's protector occurred when she was five or six. We were living at 712 Alabama Ave. Michelle had received one of those "life-size" dolls for Christmas. This particular model would "walk" with you when you held on to one hand, you could also change clothes, feed it, change diapers. You get the picture. I forgot to mention the arms and legs, actually the entire body was pretty rigid. Much too rigid by today's standards, but this was 1974 or '75.

Michelle was alternately playing with her doll, and sliding down the upstairs hall. At some point she fell on the upturned rigid hand/arm of her doll. After wiping her tears, and making sure she was okay, she continued playing, and the day went on. That night we were all asleep, when Michelle woke up the entire house with bloodcurdling screams. Janet and Michelle shared a bedroom, my bedroom was next door, and Mommy's was at the other end of the second floor. Suddenly lights were on everywhere trying to figure out what is going on!

Janet was asking what was wrong, while Mommy and I flew into the room. Michelle was inconsolable and was just crying huge tears and screaming. Michelle had tried to tell Mommy earlier that she was hurting, *now* Mommy was listening. Mommy tried to get Michelle to sit up, this only prompted more bloodcurdling screams.

We knew we had to get Michelle to the hospital. We knew something was going on inside; we just weren't sure what. Everyone quickly got dressed while Michelle continued to cry and scream! Mommy told me I was going to have carry Mickey down the stairs and out back to the car. Having already seen how much Mickey would scream just trying to get her to sit up, I knew this would not be easy.

I remember being scared that I was going to drop her. I said to Mickey, *"You have to trust me, I am not going to drop you."* I asked her, *"Do you trust me?"* She nodded as tears still streamed down her face. I remember saying to Mickey in advance, *"This is going to hurt, I'm sorry."* I still remember quite vividly the scream she let out went I picked her up. Now Mickey and I are both crying! I was never so afraid to go down a set of stairs as I was that night! I can't recall if it was Janet or Mommy, probably both, who helped guide me down the stairs. One in front of me, going down backwards facing Mickey and I, the other behind me holding my belt.

We got down the stairs and into the car, with more screams, and made it to the hospital. I was sitting in the back seat holding Mickey with Janet sitting next to me. We made it to the hospital in record time. (Michelle maintains that it was only her and Mommy who went to the hospital, and that once I got her into the car, Janet and I stayed at home.) Mommy and Janet are unsure at the chain of events. Once we arrived, the ER doctors seeing the tears and hearing the screams rushed us all in the back. After a series of x-rays and other tests, it was determined Michelle was bleeding internally. Apparently, the arm of the doll had partially punctured her stomach. Immediate surgery was scheduled!

Michelle recovered. The doll did not! I think Mommy gave it to Goodwill, or something similar.

I mentioned that Mickey and our grandmother, Mom, shared a birthday. As such, Mickey was arguably Mom's favorite grandchild. One summer, when Michelle was four or five, she was spending some time in Atlantic City. What I am about to relate is secondhand, as I was not there when it occurred. I have heard about this, however, from Mom, Mommy, and at least one aunt.

As I mentioned, Mickey was four or five when this happened. She was sitting at the breakfast table, Mom had the kitchen door open to let some air in, with the screen in place. It had been thundering and lightning earlier, but the storm had now stopped. Mom always loved the fresh smell of the air after a heavy rain.

For whatever reason, a sudden bolt of bluish light came in through the screen and encircled Mickey. It didn't touch her or hurt her in any way, but it encircled Mickey as she sat at the table. Mom was standing by the stove and initially had her backed turned to Mickey. It was when Mickey went, *"Look at the pretty light"* that Mom turned around and froze in her tracks.

Raw lightning was circling around Mickey!

Mickey raised her cereal spoon to touch the light. Mom half screamed/half bellowed in her Bajan accent, *"Don't yeh dare raise your spoon, don't move a muscle."* Mickey froze, but listened and did not raise her spoon. After what seemed like an eternity, the lightning retreated, leaving a burned screen in its place. Mom quickly shut the kitchen door.

If Michelle had raised her spoon, she would not be here now! The lightning would have surely been drawn to the spoon and her. When Mom told our mother, she could not explain where the lightning came from as the storm had passed, and why the light just circled around her before retreating. That further convinced Mom that Mickey was special.

There were several times when I would be Michelle's tormentor. As a teenager, I didn't always want to be bothered with my annoying younger sister tagging along. There were other times, when I would be left in charge when Mommy went out. I would pick at Michelle to get her to yell at me. Then I would say, "Who are you yelling at, I'm your older brother… go to your room!" Then I could watch TV or do whatever without her bothering me for a while before taking her "off punishment."

One incident that I'll never forget. I was upstairs talking to Mommy about something, asking for her advice, or something. Michelle was downstairs playing and lost track of where I was. Suddenly Mommy and I both heard Michelle yell, *"Stephen you better stop, I'm going to tell Mommy! Stephen stop!"* She didn't know that I was upstairs talking to Mommy at that very moment.

I turned to Mommy with as sincere a look as I could muster and said, *"See, Ma, I told you it's not always me! How can I be picking on her when I am right here; she is making it up!"* That incident gave me a free pass for about one week.

In true big brother fashion, I could pick on my younger sister, but no one else better pick on her! I mentioned earlier how the neighborhood pool was down the hill from our neighborhood in Valley Green. My friends and I would always go together and leave together. I mentioned how my best friend Robbie had a sister named Cheryl who was around the same age as Michelle. Occasionally we had to take them along when we went to the pool.

This one instance some older guys from Valley Green started picking on Michelle, and then Cheryl. Robbie and I confronted them first, then our friends backed us up. We did not get into a fight, but it came very close. So much so that we all got thrown out of the pool. The other boys were going to get reinforcement, so our little crew quickly left and headed up the hill to safety. We didn't visit the pool again for about three weeks!

Within our circle, our neighborhood, everyone knew that Michelle and Cheryl were our little sisters, so no one ever bothered them. In fact, everyone pretty much looked out for them if we were not around.

By the time I was seventeen, Mommy would send Michelle to round me up when we had to go somewhere. Robbie's mother would send his sister Cheryl to do the same. Oftentimes Michelle and Cheryl would play together when they would be sent to round us up. I think Michelle and Cheryl enjoyed having the "weight" of our mothers behind them. Like I said, our mothers knew pretty much where we were, we were just out of shouting distance.

We would be playing basketball in the alley over on 9th street, over Dave and Steve Dinkel's, playing football at St. E's, or just sitting around talking. Here would come Michelle and Cheryl.

The guys would start to tease us saying, "Here comes the 'Boss Squad.'" Michelle and Cheryl would stand right in the middle of our game, put their hands on their little hips and proclaim with much sass… "Mommy said you have to come home *right now!*"

It was pretty cool actually, but the guys always teased us about the "Boss Squad."

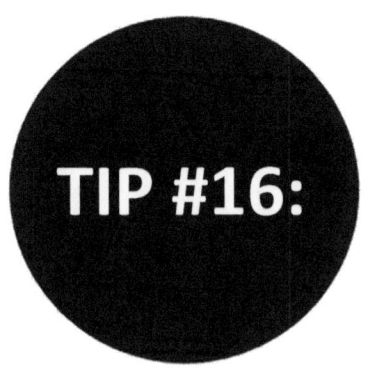

**TIP #16:**

## YOUNGER SIBLINGS
## ARE THE BEST SPIES

*I am not advocating that you encourage your children to tell, no, snitch on each other. Advocating that would establish patterns of behavior that later in life would be problematic. That said, younger siblings are the best spies a parent could have.*

*Particularly if there is a significant age difference. The reason being is simple, younger siblings watch their older siblings like a hawk. They see and know everything! At younger ages, when filters are less developed, they will blurt out the truth without a second thought. Often to the chagrin of their older sibling.*

*If you want to know the truth about something, if the details don't sound quite right... ask your youngest child. They know all the "dirt." I cannot tell you how many times I was busted because our mother questioned Michelle.*

**TIP #17:**

## BEWARE THE DOUBLE AGENT

*While younger siblings generally know all the "dirt," there are times when they may make things up in an effort to get back at an older sibling. Beware.*

# CHAPTER FOURTEEN

## "You Hear That Ambulance…That's Your Brother, Hurry and Finish Eating"

The last two years of my high school also proved to be the last two years we would live at 712 Alabama Avenue, S.E. After I began college, my mother and Michelle moved to Camp Springs, Maryland, a suburb of Washington, DC. With my sister and I now in college, I guess my mother felt it was time for a change.

In true Stephen fashion, my junior and senior years of high school were just as eventful as almost every year before them. Among the various Stephen incidents that occurred during this time; were my learning to drive, my learning that garages *DO NOT* jump out into the middle of the alley, my learning to *NOT* leave the scene of an accident, the mixing a of super strength floor cleaner that nearly killed me, and one ride in an ambulance. *WOW!* Looking back now the last two years of high school were actually pretty mild… well compared to the earlier years!

Let's talk about the super strength floor cleaner. As I stated in earlier chapters, being grounded or even being delayed going outside was a far worse form of torture than any interrogator could dream up. Among my Saturday chores before heading outside, I had to sweep and mop all the floors in the house. This meant the kitchen, the two upstairs bathrooms, and the one guest bathroom in the family room. No problem, I could usually do these in fewer than fifteen minutes. I can't attest to the quality of the job, but it was done! Well, this one particular Saturday was an important day, I cannot recall what was so special, but I knew my buddies and I had big plans.

I went to get the bucket from under the utility sink, next to the washing machine, and ran the hot/warm water for the bucket. I picked up the ammonia and noticed there was only a corner left in the bottle. Just my luck! That meant I would have to ask my mother for money, go to the corner store, buy another bottle of lemon ammonia, and *then* come back home to mop all the floors. This meant wasting valuable outdoor time. So, I had to come up with a solution… quick!

My solution, I picked up the bottle of Clorox! I figured ammonia works well by itself and bleach cleans stains… so I figured the two together…!

I did not bother to read the warning on either bottle's label, I just poured them in!

I came back a minute or two later to turn off the water and get ready to mop with my super-strength floor cleaner. Except something very strange stopped me. First, I noticed that my lungs were burning a little as I reached to turn off the running water, I also noticed a strange "cloud" hovering over the bucket. I left out of the washing area, choking and coughing as I called for my mother to come from the kitchen and see this strange cloud! My mother came, took one look and *knew* exactly what was wrong. She immediately told me to cover my nose and mouth, while she did the same.

She then grabbed the bucket, dumped the contents and ran the water to flush it down the drain. After the immediate danger was over, I guess to confirm her hunch; she asked what did I mix in the bucket? I explained that there wasn't enough ammonia, so I mixed a little Clorox with it… to make it stronger. The look on her face was like; "*LORD, please don't let me kill this boy*"??!! Again, GOD *does* look out for babies and fools!

I am not sure if my mother was more upset because of my deadly concoction, or because I had been so stupid to mix chemicals without reading the warning on the label. That was how I learned that bleach and ammonia should **_never_** be mixed together!! Fortunately for me, because there was only a small amount of ammonia in the bottle, the "cloud" was not very big or strong. Had there been more of an equal mixture, I probably would have been dead before my mother even got to me.

Years later, when my son became old enough to take over the floor cleaning duties, I was very careful to point out the warning on the ammonia and bleach labels. I also gave him strict instructions. If you are not sure, ask! **_Before_** you mix anything!

I learned how to drive late, due to my left arm having been in a cast for so many years, plus the physical therapy afterwards. I learned how to drive my senior year of high school. My cousin Richard had taught my sister, Janet, how to drive, so the task of teaching me to drive fell on him as well. For Janet learning to actually drive was easy, parking on the other hand was difficult. For me it was just the opposite, parking was a piece of cake, driving on side streets was no problem… trying to stay in my lane with other cars whizzing past me… now that was a problem! I would get rattled and start to drift over into the next lane, or in a panic let go of the steering wheel altogether. I failed to mention my cousin Richard had a brand-new 1970 something Monte Carlo. My drifting made him quite nervous, needless to say. After about three-four weeks of near misses, Richard gave me an ultimatum, he would take me out two more times, if I couldn't stay in the lanes by then I would have to find someone else to teach me. Maybe it was the pressure, or the disappointment in me by my favorite cousin. Whatever the reason, I got it together, with no further problems… until I would later drive by myself.

My mother had a 1970 something chocolate brown Oldsmobile Toronado, one of the first front wheel drive cars, and a land yacht of the first order. For a new driver, the Toronado was a lot of car to maneuver. One day I convinced my mother to let me drive to the Safeway rather than walk there, this would be the first time I would drive her car alone. After the usual cautionary warnings, I was off. The drive to and from was uneventful until I turned into the alley of our block. I chose to turn into the alley entrance just south of Portland Street, this way I turn onto the long part of the "I," come straight down and pull straight into the driveway in my back yard. Again, no problem, until I was coming down the long part of the "I" and was distracted by something just long enough for me to drive into the corner of a neighbor's wooden garage. I wasn't going fast, so it was more of crunching into the corner of the garage. The garage belonged to the old lady whose grape vine we used to rob, so since I knew she heard nothing, I backed out and continued on down the alley before stopping to check for damage. I pulled out a few pieces of crunched wood, and was pleased there was no visible or obvious damage. I parked the car in the backyard, went inside and put whatever I had purchased on the kitchen table, gave my mother the keys, thanked her, and went upstairs to my room.

Sometime later, my mother was going out somewhere. So, it was just Michelle and I, leaving me in charge. I thought I had picked out the wood chunks pretty well, apparently not, because my mother was suddenly standing in my doorway demanding for me to come outside with her. Once outside she had one question for me,

*"Why are there wood splinters sticking out of my grill and turn light?"* I really could not think of a good reason or answer, so I said, *"A garage kind of got in the way."*

My mother was now running late, said we will deal with this tomorrow and left. I could tell that she was mad, but she was very calm about the situation, which gave me plenty of reason to be concerned.

You know, I don't know what is worse, being punished immediately or having to wait for your punishment. Actually, I do know; waiting is by far more traumatic. You *KNOW* you're in trouble, and then your parents use the added psychological torment of making you wait, sometimes for a day or two or three. Just when you are *sure* that they forgot about it... wham they drop the hammer!

The next day my mother and I walked back up the alley. She wanted to see the garage that *kind of* got in the way! There was a hole about the size of three fists where the corner of the car had crunched the corner of the garage. She made me get some plastic and cover the hole, so that critters would not get inside, and that was it… or so I thought. Unknown to me, my mother later went to the old lady's house and talked to her about the damage… the old lady didn't even know I had hit her garage, and reached an agreement about repairing the damage.

I knew my mother was taking this a little too much in stride, but I could not figure what she had in store for me. I soon found out the following Saturday. I had finished my chores and was getting ready to head outside when my mother stopped me.

She said, *"Where are you going?"*

*"I said outside?!"*

My mother just as cool as ice, said, *"Oh no! You're not finished with your chores yet, come with me."*

I followed her outside and up the alley toward the garage, that had *kind of* gotten in the way. There neatly laid out was wood, nails, a hammer and saw, and several gallons of white paint. Also arranged were several folding chairs in a neat arch around the work site. I looked at her with a questioning look about the chairs. She simply said don't worry about it, get to work.

By the time I had finished measuring the wood the chairs began to fill up… with my friends…who had been invited to watch me work! My mother, Robbie's mom and the old lady provided sandwiches and drinks for my audience.

I, on the other hand, had to wait until I was finished before I could eat.

My friends were having a ball, I mean a genuine ball, at my expense! Especially after I finished the repair and was told that I had to paint the entire garage. The roar of laughter that went up was deafening! My friends left after a while, but would always find a reason to cruise back through to comment on my painting skills. For many a weekend, this particular Saturday, was the talk of the block among my friends.

I made sure to give that garage and all garages there after a wide berth when driving.

I attended St. Aloysius Gonzaga College High School, Gonzaga, as we called it. Gonzaga was an all-boys catholic school run by the Jesuit priests, in Northwest DC not far from Union Station and the Capitol Building. Right next door to Gonzaga was the Academy of Notre Dame, an all-girls high school. The two schools had one building in common that they shared, with 2/3 of it belonging to Notre Dame.

The nuns of Notre Dame fiercely guarded, and I do mean guarded the entrance to Notre Dame. Walking down the one hallway that was still Gonzaga, one came to a door, when you walked through this door you were now in the Academy of Notre Dame. Getting through this door took an act of God, and then even then you might still be questioned!

I point this out to illustrate our starvation for girls. Because Gonzaga was an all-boys school, you only saw girls at lunch if you hung by the Notre Dame lunchroom, or if you were involved in sports after school since Gonzaga and Notre Dame shared sports facilities.

The glamour sports that got all of the girl's attention were; football, basketball and track. I was too short for basketball, and too small physically to play football, so I ran track, which just happened to be co-ed. I ran relays and was a high-jumper. There were other sports, but these three were the only ones that mattered to most of my friends and I. During football and basketball season, Notre Dame provided the cheer leaders for us.

Being on the track team was nice, but the season was relatively short compared to football and basketball, and didn't carry as much "King of the Campus" appeal as the other two sports. My football dreams had ended long ago in Robbie's backyard, so I did the only other thing I could do. I became the assistant trainer my senior year. That meant I helped to tape ankles before games, cut tape off those same ankles after the game, and helped out the equipment manager. I also replaced broken chin straps or tightened face masks on the sidelines. The point is I was part of the team, and as such got some play from the girls at Notre Dame.

I was not a lady's man by any stretch of the imagination, but I still got a little play from the girls. This was largely because I could play gatekeeper to the stars of the team.

When I was in high school, Gonzaga was horrible in football. My three years there from grades 10–12, we were 1-28-1. Gonzaga in the '30s, '40s, and '50s was a football power, and they are again, but when I was there, we were simply "sorry."

Sorry or not, the football team still got the girls!

It was during one of home games that I got injured. Injured, you ask? How does an assistant trainer/assistant equipment manager get injured? Easy, if you are me! We had just lost yet another game. The players and coaches of both teams were leaving the field, as I and the other trainer and manager began to pack-up the odds and ends of the sideline. I was carrying two large trainer's boxes, by their handles, one in each hand, and began across the field.

Buchanan Field was the name of our stadium. It was a field in the sense that it was fairly large and occasionally green. By the third game of the season, most of the grass was gone in the middle of the field. After a game, there were divots everywhere on the field. Carrying two large and ungainly trainer's boxes, I was not watching where I was walking. My foot got stuck in a divot, and the rest as they say is history. I unceremoniously lost what little balance I had carrying the two boxes. I sprawled across the ground, with one box falling open, and me cracking my chin HARD on the other metal box. My ankle hurt so much from the fall, I thought that I had fractured it or twisted it… actually it was my chin (no pun) that took it the hardest. The other trainer and manager came running out to me, as did one or two cheerleaders. I am laying one the ground, part embarrassed and part in pain!

Someone went and got a few of the coaches. By the time the coaches arrived I was sitting up, and was able to walk with only a slight limp, but my chin was killing me! I was helped to the locker room where they elevated my ankle and placed ice on it. I was also given an icepack for my chin. Of course, the players, many of whom were my buddies, were wondering what had happened to me! I was in too much pain from my chin, and too embarrassed to try to explain. I remember hearing the head coach say; "No wonder we can't win a game, we can't even keep our trainers healthy."

At some point the decision was made to call for an ambulance and to contact my mother. The closest hospital to Gonzaga is Washington Hospital Center, where I was born. Normally the ambulance would transport to the closest hospital, but because my injuries were not life-threatening, and because it was 1976, the ambulance agreed to transport to my mother's choice of hospital. The ride from Gonzaga to Washington Hospital Center by ambulance is maybe ten to twelve minutes. My mother chose to have me transported to Greater Southeast Community Hospital, a ride of maybe thirty to thirty-five minutes by ambulance. Why, you ask? My mother was home with Michelle, Janet was in college, and the ambulance route to Greater Southeast Community Hospital passed *right in front* of our house on Alabama Avenue!

My mother got off the telephone, finished fixing dinner, and called Michelle to eat. Remember now, my mother was a seasoned veteran of many Stephen emergencies… this was just one of the many. My mother estimated the amount of time it would take for the ambulance to travel across town, even with sirens and lights blazing.

At some point as she and Michelle were eating, my mother began to hear a siren nearing our house, at just about the expected time. My mother said those now famous words to Michelle;

*"You hear that ambulance… that's your brother, hurry and finish eating!"*

My mother timed it perfectly! She and Michelle pulled up into the Emergency entrance, just as they began to unload me from the back of the ambulance. This part I'll never forget, my mother runs up to me, not knowing the extent of my injuries and does what most mothers would do. She goes to caress my face and chin… only my chin hurts… a lot!

I was seeing stars, moons, asteroids, you name it! I was trying to let my mother know that she was causing me severe pain. I was squirming but was unable to speak because she was *holding* my chin. I think it was one of the ambulance attendants who told her that she might want to let go of my chin, as it was one of my injuries!

It was determined by the ER doctors that I suffered a mild sprain to my ankle. My chin, however, was severely bruised along with a nice sized bone chip to the lower jaw.

To this day, I think I am the only assistant trainer/equipment manager to ever get injured in the history of Gonzaga High School. Did I tell you that Gonzaga opened its doors in 1821?

*For parents of teen-age accident-prone children refer to tips:*

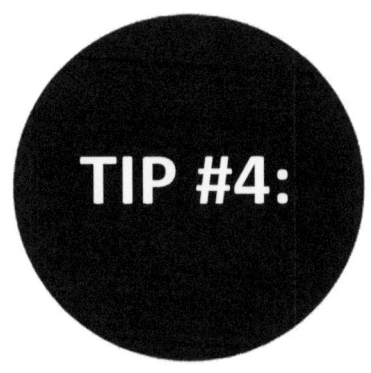

**KEEP CALM AND CARRY ON**

**BE PATIENT, LET YOUR CHILD
TELL ON THEMSELVES**

# CHAPTER FIFTEEN

## Cousin Richard

Richard Anthony Cook, is the youngest of three sons born to my Aunt Elease and Uncle Bill in Atlantic City, New Jersey. Growing up, Richard was part of the group of cousins who were "ahead" of me, as a result I was seen as too young to "hang" with them.

In spite of this, Richard, who is ten years older than me, always made time to stop by and see how I was doing whenever I came to Atlantic City. To this day, Richard calls me *Wild Man* because of all my accidents and mishaps.

All of my cousins are family, and I love them dearly, but Richard soon became my favorite male cousin. Anyone who comes from a family with lots of cousins knows what I mean when I talk about having a favorite cousin. Perhaps it is because he is the youngest of his brothers, or because he was among the youngest of their group of cousins, whatever the reason Richard always made time for me. I have always viewed Richard more as the big brother I never had, than as just strictly a cousin.

After graduating from Atlantic City High School, Richard enrolled at Norfolk State University (NSU), in Norfolk, Virginia. It was a big deal for Richard to go to NSU, because both of his brothers enlisted in the Navy after high school. Uncle Bill, for that matter, had also served in the Navy. Years later Richard and I were sitting around, talking about nothing, somehow the topic came up of the military. It was then that I learned that Richard and I shared a similar view. While we both understand the importance of the military, and appreciate the sacrifice of those who have served, we just knew that it was not for either of us.

Aunt Elease, whom we called Aunt "Leasie" and Uncle Bill were both heavy smokers. I point this out not to criticize, or pass judgement, but to set up a story. I have never smoked... anything, and this next story is probably a large reason why. Richard was finishing up a year at Norfolk State, I can't recall if it was his freshman or sophomore year. Nonetheless, Aunt Leasie and Uncle Bill were driving down from Atlantic City to pick him up. Since Washington, DC is on the way, they stopped at our house for a while. When I heard they were driving down to pick up Richard, I begged Mommy to let me go. My mother said yes, and Aunt Leasie and Uncle Bill said yes, talk about some kind of happy!!!

That happiness soon faded. The drive from DC to Norfolk is about 2 hours. I mentioned that Aunt Leasie and Uncle Bill were heavy smokers... correction... they were chain smokers. That meant that before one cigarette burnt out, they used the last bit to light a new cigarette! Mind you I am in the back seat... dying... from the cigarette smoke in the car. Uncle Bill, who I mentioned before was my godfather, was also very funny about his cars. He always liked "big cars," fully loaded! I think it was an Oldsmobile Ninety-Eight Regency he had, power windows, the works, and air conditioning.

I don't know how it looked from the outside, maybe not too bad since the A/C was on full blast, but I was dying from all the cigarette smoke. I swear you could cut the smoke with a knife! I tried to crack one of the windows in the back to let some fresh air in, and some smoke out. I think I had maybe a minute of reprieve before Uncle Bill realized and closed my window. Fussing at me for letting his A/C out!! Really A/C is what you're concerned about Uncle Bill?

Of course, I kept that thought to myself.

Eventually we arrived on the campus of NSU, and at Richard's dorm. I think I half rolled out, half fell out of the back seat when we parked. FRESH AIR!!!! Of course, there was the return trip. By the time we got back to DC to drop me off, Richard was also dying from the smoke. He asked his parents if he could stay in DC for a few days and then catch the Greyhound. To this day I have never smoked... anything. I am pretty sure if there was any curiosity, that trip to NSU squashed all of those thoughts. Both Aunt Leasie and Uncle Bill have gone on now, every now and then when Richard and I start reminiscing, the trip to NSU always comes up.

After Richard finished at Norfolk State, he came to live with us in DC at 712 Alabama Ave. S.E. Richard took over what was Janet and Michelle's room, as Janet was away at college. Michelle and Mommy shared a bedroom. This would turn out to a pivotal time for me as I was entering junior high school. As I mentioned earlier, my father was not around shortly after the divorce. It was Richard who kept me from going sideways. I was a teenager, who was tired of taking orders from women (Mommy, Sissy, Mom), and was starting to rebel a little. Richard kept me in check. Sometimes he would just talk to me, other times he would "tighten me up" while giving boxing lessons on how to hold my guard. Some of those accidental punches that were just a little too hard, I am sure were not accidental. He was just letting me know...

Two things of significance happened when I started junior high school. I got a job delivering the *Washington Post* newspaper, and I began to steal. The route that I had delivering the Washington Post began maybe six blocks from our house on Alabama Ave, requiring me to cross Martin Luther King Blvd and go down the hill on Portland Street. All in all, it wasn't a hard job, it required me to get up super early to meet my "drop-off" manager, deliver my papers, and then head onto school... across town. Saturdays and Sundays were a little easier, because they were not school days. The biggest challenge was getting paid. You see in those days, you had to deliver the papers, and then once a week to collect payment from your customers. After I collected from everyone, I turned the money into my "drop-off" manager, who in turn gave me my portion.

The problem came when people didn't pay, or had whatever excuse, as why they were short that week. I still had to turn in whatever monies I collected, but if everyone didn't pay, there wasn't enough for me to get paid as well. Often times I would have to go two weeks before I got paid. I would get my back pay also, but it was always such a hassle. I use to hate collection day! I think after 9 months; I quit!

The junior high school I attended was still in our old neighborhood in Northwest Washington. With us now living in Southeast, Janet and I had to catch three city buses to go across town. We would catch the "A2," "A4" or "A6" into downtown DC then walk two to three blocks to catch our next bus. On a good day I could cut it down to just two buses, but if I missed this one particular bus, then it was back to three buses.

In junior high school, I met one other student from my class who also lived in southeast. Now I had something to look forward to riding across the city. The stealing started off small. My friend and I would go into the People's Drugstore (before CVS bought them out) while waiting for our transfer bus. We would go into the school supply section and would snatch a package of pens when no one was looking, sometime we would take a package of notebook paper. In DC during the winter, everyone is wearing big heavy coats with scarfs, so no one suspected… or so we thought.

We didn't steal every day, and usually would pay for what we had, but every now and then for the thrill of it… we would steal. One day it occurred to us, instead of just snatching school supplies, what about snacks for our long bus ride? You weren't supposed to eat or drink on the bus, but if you sat way in the back the driver couldn't see you. One day we almost got caught, as we were stuffing a 2-pack of Krispy Kreme Glazed Jelly donuts inside our coats. We pretended like we were adjusting our backpacks and had just finished stuffing the donuts inside our coats when the manager turned the corner.

He looked at us, and we looked at him. He was looking at us so hard, we just knew we were busted. Instead, he said something like, *"Backpacks too heavy?"* He didn't check our backpacks, pat us down or anything. We said something like, *"Yeah, just adjusting them a little."* We hurriedly left, once outside we quickly walked around the corner and nervously laughed, as we realize how close we came to being caught.

After that incident we steered clear of the People's drugstore for a few weeks, and stopped stealing altogether. I guess you could say, "We were scared straight" … long before the actual reform program of the same name.

During junior high school, electric football sets were all the rage. It was an electric table painted to look like a football field, with a cardboard grandstand, and two teams loosely painted to look like actual NFL teams. My friends in junior high school started our own league, and took thing to the next level.

We would use model car paint to paint our teams to improve upon their appearance. We would use an unfolded paperclip to paint stripes and numbers of our favorite players. We would have a defense and offense, instead of the standard eleven players that came with each set. We would go through the yellow pages, cut out last names and glue them on in thin strips on the back of our player's jerseys. Finally, we would glue steel nuts to the underside of our defensive and offensive lines to increase their pushing power. We were serious!

Some of us were better painters than others, so we would "order" our favorite team, in home or away jerseys, and then pay for them. It became a cottage industry at Rabaut Junior High school. An average "custom" set might cost $15–$20. Big money for junior high school kids in the early '70s! I no longer had my paperboy route, so I began to "borrow" from my mother, and eventually my cousin Richard.

I would wait until Richard would go to take a shower in the morning, and then quickly sneak into his room and "borrow" a $10 dollar bill. At this age, I had no concept that adults *knew* how much money was in their wallet or purse. I just figured it would go unnoticed… it didn't! It was noticed!

Apparently, my mother and Richard had been noticing this for a while, and had discussed a plan to stop me once and for all. When asked about the new set of football players I had, I would simply say my friend and I traded, or something similar. One day Richard went to take his morning shower, or so I thought. I snuck into his room, but his wallet wasn't in its usual place. I am looking around for his wallet, when I hear what sounded like the voice of God! "Looking for this?'

I turned around, there was my cousin Richard holding his wallet, and my mother was standing behind him. Let's just say I escaped the death sentence… but just barely! I didn't go to school that day! Besides the epic spanking, I think I was grounded for one full month. Just school and home, nothing else!

I have never, ever, stolen anything since.

Like I said, Richard was more like big brother to me, and apart from the times he was keeping me on the straight and narrow, or tightening me up, we hung out. My mother, as part of her work as Regional Director for the Boys and Girls club, would often get tickets to the Washington Bullets basketball games. She would get enough so that Richard could bring one of his buddies, and I could bring my best friend Robbie. We had some good times! Richard sometimes bought a buddy, other times his girlfriend. They used to get a kick watching me and Robbie rooting for our favorite Bullets player, to the point of getting hoarse.

Later on, as I got older, Richard would give me the "birds and bee" talk. He would tell me how I should treat a lady, among other things. Richard and I were just cool! I could ask him just about anything, and always gave me real answers.

To this day, Richard and I remain extremely close. I served as a groomsman at his first wedding. He was best man at mine. After his marriage Richard moved to suburban Maryland. As an adult, I would go over to his house and hangout, and help him with projects. When I had my son, Richard became a big brother to him.

Richard has had some hardships, so have I. Through it all we kept talking to each other, encouraging each other. I can honestly say, if it were not for my cousin Richard, things could have ended up very differently for me. According to all the statistics, a young man growing up in a single parent home, a single mother with three children, in Southeast DC, I am supposed to be dead or in prison! Richard said, "Not on my watch!" I love you man!

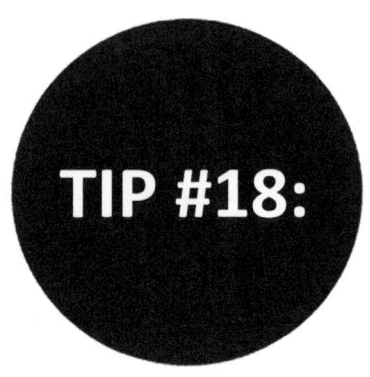

## IT TAKES A VILLAGE

*This is true for all single parents, but it has particular significance for single mothers raising teenage sons. Single fathers raising daughters face similar challenges, however, the societal ramifications are not as severe.*

*As a single mother, there will come a time when your son will grow tired of "taking orders" from a woman. Add in the fact that the majority of teachers are female, giving orders throughout the school day, and you have a recipe for rebellion. In a home without a male figure, this can be magnified. Rebellion can take many forms; resentment, rudeness, defiance, or stealing.*

*Reach out to male family members or a willing neighbor, to assist you in guiding your son and provide a needed buffer for you both. An older male cousin, an uncle, a grandfather can provide the needed male perspective and bonding. Given time, "the village" will bring your son back to you, restored and back on course.*

*It will be a trying time for both you and your son, but this too shall pass.*

# CHAPTER SIXTEEN

## Devil's Food Cake

Devil's Food cake! I love Devil's Food cake! It was this love of this dark chocolate cake that caused me to lose sleep for almost three nights!

In chapter one of this book, I mentioned that 5721 Chillum Place, N.E. wasn't the first address I had lived at. It was just the address where my personal saga through life began. There is one incident; that involved Devil's Food cake that occurred at the previous address of 2024 South Dakota Street, N.E. a few months prior to us moving to Chillum Place.

My Aunt Carmen, or "Aunt Connie" as we called her, had driven down from Philadelphia, PA for the weekend. My cousin Kathy came down with her. My sister Janet is three years older than me; my cousin Kathy was maybe two years older than Janet. At some point my parents and Aunt Connie decided to go out for a while. They left seven-year-old Janet and nine-year-old Kathy in charge of four-year-old me. Remember, this was 1963, so you could still do those kinds of things!

Janet and Kathy played with Janet's dolls, while I basically got on their nerves! At some point they had enough and told me to go outside in the backyard, making sure to tell me that I could not leave the yard. While I was still outside Janet and Kathy came downstairs to the kitchen and decided to bake a cake, I assumed they had gotten permission first. They checked on me first, and then they started to mix the batter.

I had been promised I could lick one of the beaters if I behaved. As luck would have it, Janet and Kathy were making my absolute favorite... Devil's Food cake!

I was sitting on a stool, licking one of the beaters as they poured the batter into two cake pans, and carefully placed them in the oven. At this point I was ordered to stay outside while the cake was baking, so I would not make it fall. I didn't understand what they were talking about, but I knew they were baking my favorite cake... so I stayed outside! At some point Janet and Kathy took the cakes out of the oven and had placed them on cooling racks, so that they could ice them later.

I remember coming to the screen door to ask Janet and Kathy if I could come back inside. The words never even left my mouth... instead my little eyes were locked... like radar on the two Devil's Food cakes cooling on the counter. Being as quiet as a four-year-old can be, I snuck inside, took a butter knife out of the drawer and cut me a big hunk of cake. The fact that I was not allowed to play with a knife didn't matter to me at that point; I just wanted my cake! The cake was good, even without the icing. So, I cut another hunk of cake! I am saying hunks, not slices! I was four, so the concept of cutting a neat slice of cake simply didn't exist.

Now that I had my fill of Devil's Food cake, I went back outside to continue playing. At some point Janet and Kathy came downstairs, the scream they let out could have been heard all the way back in North Philadelphia. Upon hearing this scream, I did what any self-respecting four-year-old would do, I hid! Well, I tried to anyway!!

In my young life I had never seen Janet or Kathy so mad before. So, I did what any self-respecting four-year-old would do, I started to cry! Because I was crying, I didn't see Janet and Kathy talking off to the side of the kitchen. They started giving each other knowing looks and shook their heads in my direction.

They said, *"Oh! You're in trouble!"*

*"I am sure glad that I am not you right now; you're in trouble!"*

Now I started to get mad and said, *"No I'm not. It's just a cake! Mommy and Daddy won't care!"*

Janet and Kathy, both wiser and older said, *"Oh no, you don't understand, you're in BIG trouble!"*

*"Really, really BIG trouble!"*

I kept saying, no I'm not it's just a cake. The more I said that, the more they kept shaking their heads and saying that I was in really BIG trouble. Finally, my anger and defiance turned to curiosity, and then to concern. I finally asked the question that they had been hoping for… no waiting for. *"Why am I in such BIG trouble?"*

In unison they said, *"Do you know what kind of cake you just ate?"*

I replied with a little bit of concern in my voice, *"Devil's Food cake?"*

In unison they said, *"Yes and do you know why they call it Devil's Food cake?"*

By this time, most of the defiance had left me. Now I was concerned and just a little bit frightened, but I was still trying to be brave when I said, *"N-n-n-o-o! Why?"*

Like two sharks smelling blood, Janet and Kathy went for the kill. They said, *"It is called Devil's Food cake because if you eat too much at one time, when you go to bed at night… you turn into a devil!"* And if that was not enough, they added, *"It lasts for two days!"*

I countered with a typical four-year-old response. I put my hand to my ears, closed my eyes and kept saying; *"No, it doesn't, no it doesn't!"*

Eventually the test of wills ended, I stuck my tongue out and went back outside to play, forgetting all about their warnings.

My parents and Aunt Connie returned sometime later. As dinner was being prepared, I received a stern talking to (for not minding Janet and Kathy), but that was all! Seeing Janet and Kathy standing in the background giggling, I stuck my tongue out at them. We all ate dinner, played a board game or two, and then it was time for us kids to go to bed.

Bedtime! Oh no bedtime! All of a sudden, I remembered *ALL* of Janet and Kathy's earlier warnings. At that point I made up my mind. I was **NOT** going to bed!

The struggle, the screaming, the crying that ensued, you would have thought someone was trying to kill me… which from my point of view that was exactly what they were trying to do! I was not going to bed! I was not going to turn into a devil!

My father, mother, and Aunt Connie were unaware of what Janet and Kathy had told me earlier in the day with regards to me eating their precious cake. All they knew is that they had a seriously hysterical four-year-old on their hands. I was letting out bloodcurdling screams, hyperventilating with tears just streaming down his face, and a "death grip" on the stair railing. I was not letting go of that railing for anything!

After what seemed like forever, but in reality was probably a minute or less, the struggle ended. My father, mother, and Aunt Connie were standing around looking at each other like; "What is going on here?" I am sitting on the first step, still with my "death grip" on the railing. I remember my father turning to Janet and Kathy, who were standing nearby to ask if they knew what was going on.

I believe they said something like, *"I don't know; just crazy I guess?"* and *"I guess he ate too much cake."*

My mother, this time said, "Come on, Steve, it's time for bed." The minute I heard the "b" word I started screaming and crying again, and I tightened my grip on the railing! Just seeing this reaction from me, everyone knew that something was up!

Again, Janet and Kathy were questioned, although I cannot recall by whom. Again, they claimed ignorance to the reason for this living room drama that was unfolding.

Now it was Aunt Connie's turn to try to get me to go to bed. Again, the same reaction, the same bloodcurdling screams, and the same river of tears! After what seemed an eternity of asking me; "What was wrong?" and getting no answer, I was finally able to utter a single word.

*"Scared!"*

My father was now fussing at me for being scared, while my mother and Aunt Connie were trying to calm me. I remember my mother and Aunt Connie saying that they would go upstairs with me. Even with that offer, it wasn't enough. I was not going to bed! I was not going to turn into a devil!

My mother and Aunt Connie eventually were able to convince me to let go of the railing and to sit on the sofa so they could talk to me. I was still hyperventilating and crying. Between sobs and gasps I was able to say: *"Janet and Kathy told me…"* before I broke into tears again.

My father took Janet and Kathy into the kitchen and demanded they tell him what was going on. I don't know what he said to them, or what threats were made, but in a few minutes, he walked back into the living room with a thoroughly disgusted look on his face.

*"Gwen, Carmen"* he said! *"You will not believe what these two girls told this boy!"*

*"They told him he was going to turn into a devil when he went to bed, because he ate their Devil's Food Cake!"*

My mother and Aunt Connie were now looking at Janet and Kathy in total disbelief. I on the other hand was a believer! Just hearing my father's explanation to my mother and Aunt Connie sent me into hysterics… again!!

All three adults were now trying to calm me, and tell me that it was not true what Janet and Kathy told me. I wasn't buying it! The screams and crying just got stronger. This went on for quite some time. Every time they thought they had me calmed down enough to suggest going upstairs, just the mention of "upstairs" led to more tears and more hysterics.

Eventually, it was decided I could stay up with the adults downstairs. This seemed to work, as I was able to watch TV and eat ice cream. Eventually, I got drowsy and my father attempted to carry me upstairs to my bedroom. I say attempted because my survival instinct (even though I didn't know what a survival instinct was) was in full blown survival mode. Just the simple act of someone touching me, to pick me up lead to a new round of tears and screams.

Eventually the will of a four-year-old was no match for "Mr. Sandman" I don't know who carried me upstairs. All I remember is waking up the next morning with my mother lying next to me. The very first thing I did was to feel if a tail or horns had grown overnight. Whew! I was lucky, none had grown in!

Feeling quite proud of myself, I proceeded (in a most annoying way) to tell Janet and Kathy that they were wrong, that nothing happened. Janet and Kathy being very cool about it held up two fingers and said, *"It lasts for two days!"*

The bedtime drama occurred again for a second night!

On the third night Janet and Kathy graciously released me from "the curse."

I still love Devil's Food Cake… I just don't eat a lot of it anymore… you can never be too careful!

**TIP #19:**

## OLDER SIBLINGS WILL BE CRUEL

*Siblings can and will be cruel to one another, it goes without saying. Sometimes it is just for amusement, other times it is for retribution. This occasional cruelty will occur regardless of how otherwise harmonious the relationship is normally.*

*There is little you can do as a parent to prevent it. It is simply a part of growing up with siblings. Be prepared to comfort and soothe frazzled nerves and tears. This too shall pass.*

# CHAPTER SEVENTEEN

## Sissy

Sissy was my cousin, but more importantly, Sissy was my Godmother. A term that I continued to use until her death, and is a term I will continue to use when I refer to her.

Family members often asked me why I continued to refer to Sissy as my Godmother, even when I was grown and clearly able to take care of myself. I still referred to Sissy as my Godmother because I respected the love, compassion, guidance, and the closeness we continued to share throughout her life. Later in life, I moved to California. To be sure, time and distance, with me being in California, made it difficult to stay in touch, but when we did connect, we picked up as though there had been no time lapse.

Sissy's given name was Ulrica Greenridge. To her cousins and adult friends, she was Ricki. I am not sure how she came to be called Sissy by my generation. Sissy and my mother grew up together in Atlantic City, New Jersey. My mother lived on Arctic Avenue, and Sissy lived on Lexington Avenue (which is no longer remains). Growing up they were family, friends, and at times rivals, but mostly they were family! Atlantic City in the 1930s and 1940s was in many ways an even smaller town, than it is today. Especially for its Black residents! For most, the future meant graduating from Atlantic City High School and then pursue one of three main options; join the military, get a government job or go to work at one of the many hotels as a cook/chef or housekeeper. Sissy and my mother were among the few who had other ideas.

My mother enrolled at Howard University in Washington, DC, Sissy enrolled at Morgan State College (now University) in Baltimore, Maryland. Both schools are among the elite in terms of Historically Black Colleges and Universities (HBCUs). Sissy later enrolled at Howard University and earned a Master's degree in Social Work. To the best of my knowledge, I believe they were the only two from their generation in our family to head off to four-year colleges/universities, and leave Atlantic City. I believe one or two may have gone to trade schools or junior colleges in the area. Sissy like my mother entered into the education field, with Sissy spending over thirty years in the Baltimore City Public Schools as a Social Worker.

Growing up we (my mother and two sisters) lived in DC, and Sissy and her son Jeffrey lived in Baltimore, which is approximately a forty- to forty-five-minute drive in either direction. It was nothing for us to drive there for dinner, or for them to drive down from Baltimore. Often after church on Sunday, one of us would wind up at the other's home. If we weren't at each other's homes, we were here in AC visiting family. I was fortunate to have three strong women who took various roles in raising me; Mommy, Sissy, and my grandmother "Mom." They kept me and Jeff on the straight and narrow.

Sissy was tough, she brooked little foolishness. Between my mother and Sissy, attending college was never really an option. It was never a matter of "if," it was just a matter of "where." Sissy was tough but she could also be incredibly funny. There was one time the truly stands out in my memory, from the many moments.

Growing up it was rare to go shopping for new clothes with your parents, usually new clothes just showed up laying across your bed, like magic. There was this one rare time when Jeff, myself, I can't recall if Janet and Michelle were there, they probably were. Michelle would have been little like four or five, and of course Mommy and Sissy, we went to this store called C-Mart outside of Baltimore. I don't know if C-Mart still exists?

Before there was Ross, TJ Maxx, etc. there was C-Mart.

Jeff and I were in our young teens, and we found a couple of girls that we were trying to talk to. Sissy saw us, I can't recall if Mommy saw us or not. Anyway, Sissy decided she was going to be funny. Talk about shutting us down!!!

Sissy yelled out, I mean just all loud and wrong and across the store, for everyone to hear, *"Hey, Jeff what size drawers do you wear again?"*

At first we tried to ignore her and act like she wasn't talking to us. Sissy saw this and would not let up, *"Hey, you two. I know you hear me, don't act like you don't. You wearing the... (as she identified the clothes we each where wearing.)"*

After her comments, Jeff and I had to walk away from the girls. There was absolutely no comeback, no explanation... we just had to walk away. Sissy, and by this time Mommy, had a good laugh, I mean they were just rollin' over our embarrassment and frustration.

Growing up, Jeff and I were like brothers, and spent a lot of time together, especially during the summer. For that matter; Jeff, Joe, Chunky and I were all like brothers growing up, we were all cousins, but we spent so much time together that we were like brothers. Then time, life and distance took over. However, whenever we all get together, a good time is for sure!

The first and one of the few times (possibly the only time) I went fishing was when Sissy took me and Jeff to some park or lake outside of Baltimore. I don't know if you all remember, but there used to be this guy who came on TV advertising all sort of kitchen gadgets, "they sliced, they diced" they did everything but cook the meal. One product that came out was the Popeil Pocket Fisherman, it was a folding fishing rod that could fit into your back pocket. It was a big deal when they came out, well Sissy brought two, one each for me and Jeff. We couldn't wait to go fishing.

The day came, we went to this park, and Sissy helped Jeff and I put worms on our hooks and cast the line. Jeff caught two or three small fish, none of them keepers. I was getting frustrated because I caught a few but they kept getting off my line, and then I caught the big one, or so I thought. I just knew I had caught a whale, of course Sissy laughed when I told her that. Anyway, I pulled… it pulled, I pulled… it pulled, I just knew I had something big on my line. Finally, with Sissy's help I got it in… I caught a Dixie cup full of lake water!!

I had hooked the cup by the mouth, so every time I pulled, water rushed in causing the counter pull. We all had a good laugh over that.

Jeff and I with Sissy's help built a clubhouse, we helped Sissy plant a garden, we did so many things together. If you have ever been to Sissy's house there are three or four steps, you have to step down from where you park to enter through the kitchen. The original stairs had to be replaced, and Sissy found some plan in Redbook, Home & Garden, one of those magazines. Anyway, Sissy, Jeff and I built the new steps. The first time any of us had every built steps! Those steps lasted a long time, before they eventually had to be replaced, this time professionally. We went to Orioles games. I think we saw the Colts before they left Baltimore.

As a child, and sometimes as a young man in my twenties, I got into my mother's doghouse, Sissy on many occasions helped get me out of that doghouse. When I moved to California, Sissy and I kept in touch, though not as often. Funny of all the things we did when I was growing up, Sissy would often mention those stairs that we built together. In fact, I had actually forgotten about them until Sissy brought it up. Those steps made a lasting impression on her, or maybe it was just the time spent together finishing the project.

I completed a doctoral program at California State University, San Bernardino in December 2017. Before I enrolled, I talked with my sisters, my mother, my girlfriend at the time, and of course Sissy, to get their opinions. As I started my final year of coursework in September 2016, I would call Sissy, and remind her that I expected her to come out to California for my graduation. I knew that Sissy wasn't big on flying, so we kept talking about it, giving her time to get her mind right. Finally, after months of cajoling, I got Sissy to commit to coming for my graduation. Yeah!!

I knew that Sissy had been in and out of the hospital and had talked to her on many occasions. Including the next-to-last time, I called her while she was still in the hospital, she was complaining about the food, and her being ready to be released, so I knew she feeling better.

I found out on March 8, 2017 that she had just been released yet again. I talked with Jeff in the morning on March 8 and then briefly that same evening. Because of the time difference, I knew it was too late to call, and planned to call Sissy when I got home from work Thursday evening on March 9.

I found out while driving into work Thursday morning that Sissy had passed away early Thursday morning. My intended phone call was too late!

I didn't stay at work that day. Somehow, I drove back home.

Well, I guess that is one way of getting out of flying across country. Sissy, now you don't have to worry about flying across country. Now you have the best set of wings there are! While Sissy was not physically at my graduation, I knew that she was there in spirit.

I miss you, Sissy. You will always be my Godmother.

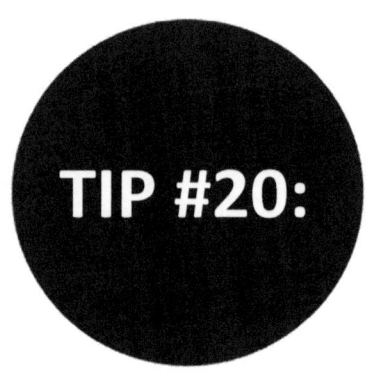

# TIP #20:

## IT TAKES A VILLAGE, PART II

*In **tip #18**, I referred to the challenges of raising an opposite gender child in a single-parent home. I highlighted the challenges of being a single mother raising a teenage male because of the increased societal ramifications. Being a single father, raising a teenage daughter can be equally challenging.*

*In the absence of a consistent or quality opposite gender role model, look to your family for support, even if that person is the same gender as you, the parent. The key point here, is simply having someone other than you that your child can turn to, or confide in. Someone who can provide the occasional buffer when necessary.*

*This is not a knock or referendum on your ability to relate to your own child. It is a simple truth: the teenage years are hard on everyone. There is no fault in asking for help, the fault is needing help and not asking for it. This too shall pass!*

# EPILOGUE

I have now reached the end of my story. It has taken me sixteen years to complete this, not because it was hard. On the contrary, I enjoyed this! These were incidents and events I haven't thought about in years, in fact as I began to write they would come back to me so vividly. As though they just happened yesterday.

So, what took so long you ask; life, divorce, work, grad school… three times! As you can tell from reading, growing up Stephen was a challenge unto itself. I was not a bad kid, just mischievous. I was not a mean-spirited kid, just guilty of lacking in good judgment from time to time… okay many times!

I share these tales with the many parents, grandparents, aunts and uncles out there of accident-prone children, to let you know that there IS hope! In these pages you may have recognized your son or daughter, or grandchild, or nephew or niece… it is OKAY… this too shall pass! Fear not your loved one will emerge into adulthood, with most of his or her faculties intact and functioning, and by most accounts be able to lead a normal and productive life. I did!

Before I moved into administration, I taught middle school for eleven years. From time to time, when time would permit, I would share with my students some of my many exploits as a child their age.

They never ceased to be amazed that Mr. Franklin was a crazy kid, and that he too did dumb stuff. These little sessions, where I would allow them a peek into my world, went onto build strong rapports with my students. Perhaps that is why I was able to push them a little harder than other teachers and get more out of them with minimal complaints. I had earned "cool points" in their eyes.

I mentioned at the beginning of this book, that my mother was (still is) a very good cook, I was just a picky eater. My being a picky eater was a virtual nightly occurrence. Between my many injuries and my "non-eating," family friends, aunts, uncles, etc. often wondered if I would make-it.

My mother tried almost everything to get me to eat in a timely manner. Even to giving my smaller portions of particular foods that I REALLY didn't like, all to no avail. I heard countless lectures about the starving children in China, blah, blah; blah... Eventually to deal with my "non-eating" self my mother developed "The Clock." For you parents who have a non-eating child listen closely.

Michelle, my youngest sister would eat just about anything. Janet, my oldest sister was semi-picky, but she never went on "The Clock" for not eating. I, however, was in a league of my own when it came to being picky! Conventional wisdom suggests, that if you have one item on your plate that you don't like, eat it first, so that you can erase that taste with the remaining food that you liked.

That was conventional wisdom, not Stephen wisdom.

My view was to delay eating the dreaded food as long as possible, often times until it was the last food item on the plate, which also meant it was the coldest item on the plate. I would often be the last person sitting at the dining table, as Janet and Michelle had finished and had been excused. Janet and several of my friends would be amazed at the saga that was playing out at the table. I was determined not to eat, and my mother was determined that I would eat; of course, she held the upper hand. "The Clock," literally an alarm clock, would come out after she got tired of fussing at me for not eating. She would give me a certain amount of time to finish eating and would set the clock to ring an alarm. She would then get up and leave me there. Throwing the food away was not an option, and she would take our pet dog "J.B." with her, so that I could not feed him.

Time would pass, the food was not being eaten, the alarm would ring and time would be up. She would come downstairs, see my plate, take me upstairs and give me a spanking. After the spanking I would be sent back downstairs to the same plate, "The Clock" would be reset to a shorter amount of time, and again she would leave. It was during one of these "Clock" sessions that I learned peas and carrots float…in the toilet.

It usually only took one "Clock" cycle to get me to finish my plate! However, on some extreme episodes it might take two or three cycles (usually when liver and onions, or okra, or string beans, or baked sweet potatoes, or black-eyed peas, or squash, or chili spaghetti were part of the meal). The exception to "The Clock" rule was Friday night. My mother would not argue with me, she would just take my plate and place it in the refrigerator. You can guess what my Saturday breakfast was! If I wanted to go outside… and if I took too long, I was grounded for the day!

The point to all of this is your child will not starve. No matter how stubborn he or she might be, no matter how picky they might be, they will NOT starve themselves! They will eat enough to keep alive and to continue to grow normally!

In those moments when you give in and say fine, you can get up but you get nothing else to eat tonight… be wary if they ask, can they get a glass of water.

They are not just drinking water… they are adding about 4 teaspoons of sugar and drinking it… or so I've been told.

Your child will survive their childhood, and yes, miracles still happen!!

www.ingramcontent.com/pod-product-compliance
Lightning Source LLC
Chambersburg PA
CBHW051204120626
46547CB00012B/1194

* 9 7 9 8 8 9 3 8 9 5 2 1 6 *